Praise for *Simple and Delicious Vegan*

"I have been following Ela for years and love everything she creates. Her recipes and photography are just beautiful. I love the visual imagery in this book, it is a must-have for anyone looking to incorporate more vegan meals!"

—Francesca Bonadonna, author of *Plantiful*

"This fantastic book is vegan cooking for everyone!"

—Alice Mary Alvarez, author of *Vegans Save the World* and *Green Homekeeping*

"What an incredible book to have in your kitchen! Filled to the brim with tasty and easy recipes like sauces, cheese and bread this is a must have for every one—vegan and not! The photos are stunning and bring her recipes to life. It will give anyone the motivation and incentive to cook from scratch to make tasty and delicious meals!"

—Sarah Kermalli, food photographer, stylist, and recipe developer

SIMPLE *and* DELICIOUS VEGAN

For permission requests, please contact the publisher at:
Mango Publishing Group
2850 S Douglas Road, 4th Floor
Coral Gables, FL 33134 USA
info@mango.bz

For special orders, quantity sales, course adoptions and corporate sales, please email the publisher at sales@mango.bz. For trade and wholesale sales, please contact Ingram Publisher Services at customer.service@ingramcontent.com or +1.800.509.4887.

Simple and Delicious Vegan: 100 Vegan and Gluten-Free Recipes Created by ElaVegan

Library of Congress Cataloging-in-Publication number: 2022940903
ISBN: (hardcover) 978-1-68481-140-3, (ebook) 978-1-68481-141-0
BISAC category code: CKB125000, COOKING / Vegan

Printed in the United States of America

SIMPLE *and* DELICIOUS VEGAN

100 Vegan and Gluten-Free Recipes
Created by ElaVegan

MICHAELA VAIS @ELAVEGAN

CORAL GABLES

This book is dedicated to my dear sister, Katrin,
who inspired me to stop eating meat at the age of six.

CONTENTS

INTRODUCTION

I'm Ela, a passionate food blogger, photographer, recipe creator, and writer who loves to cook healthy, vegan, and gluten-free food and share it with the world. I was born and raised in Germany and moved to the Dominican Republic in 2003, where I live with my partner, three cats, and several chickens!

In 2015, my creativity and love for food led me to Instagram, where I began sharing my passion for delicious and healthy plant-based dishes. At first, I posted the recipes in the Instagram captions, but as my "Instagram family" grew, so did the requests for a food blog to bundle all my recipes in a single searchable location.

By the end of 2016, my blog *ElaVegan* went live, and it turned out to be more successful than I could have ever imagined. Not only has my community grown to a thriving 1.2 million followers (and counting), but as a bonus, I've helped many people with their transition to veganism, which is a cause near and dear to my heart.

For many years, veganism suffered from a poor reputation for being restrictive and likened to "rabbit food." Not only is this objectively not true, but it's easier than ever to turn to veganism in 2023, and I continue to prove this on *ElaVegan*.

With my love for hearty, wholesome, and comforting meals, you'll never be left lacking when you use my recipes. Instead, I love sharing recipes packed with flavor (thanks to pantry-friendly herbs and spices) and good-for-you ingredients that will keep you satisfied until your next meal without weighing you down.

———

As far back as 2019, I started receiving messages, comments, and emails from my community asking about a potential cookbook. Well, better late than never—my first cookbook is finally here!

I named it *Simple and Delicious Vegan* because of my focus on allergy-friendly recipes and easy-to-find ingredients. Not only is every recipe 100 percent vegan (meat-free, fish-free, dairy-free, egg-free) and gluten-free, but they're also sometimes nut-free, corn-free, soy-free, or contain ingredient substitutions to adjust them to your dietary needs.

Living the island life here in the Dominican Republic, I also have limited access to many store-bought vegan products found elsewhere. This means I love creating my own staples like vegan mozzarella (page 51) and gluten-free wraps (page 52). I also focus heavily on creating inclusive, pantry-friendly recipes that you can enjoy worldwide.

Enjoying vegan food needn't be a struggle, no matter your dietary requirements. My plan has always been, first and foremost, to create delicious food. It just happens to be vegan! So whether you're already vegan, vegetarian, flexitarian, or your interest in vegan food has just begun, I'm hoping I can inspire you with my recipes.

MY JOURNEY TO VEGANISM

As a child, I always loved animals. I grew up with all kinds of pets: cats, dogs, rabbits, guinea pigs, mice, and more. My mom also used to take my sister and me for regular walks in a park where we could see animals like wild boars, deer, bison, birds, and so on. I always wanted to go to all the animals, pet them, take pictures of them, etc.

Together with my sister, I stopped eating meat when I was just six years old. Our shared love of animals helped us understand that it's not right to eat them. However, it was only many years later, in September 2011, that I fully transitioned to veganism and haven't looked back since.

At the time, I was suffering from severe adult acne. I'd turned to all the potential remedies I could think of to cure the skin condition, but never even considered veganism. How could I when I believed I'd *never* be able to give up cheese and dairy?!

My skin despair was so intense, though, that I eventually took the plunge and removed all dairy from my diet. Within a few months, lo and behold, my acne disappeared! And it turns out I didn't miss dairy as much as I thought I would.

Shortly after, I started to pay more attention to the vegan lifestyle and turned to documentaries to increase my knowledge. The combination of information about animal suffering (even for dairy!) and the impact of non-vegan diets on our planet broke my heart.

From that moment on, I'm 100 percent convinced that going vegan was (and still is) the best decision I've ever made. I am now proudly an ethical vegan, loving that I am both reducing the amount of suffering and destruction in the world and helping people embrace veganism by sharing delicious plant-based recipes.

I can't imagine eating any other way. Veganism isn't a diet for me—it is a complete lifestyle transition that has changed me in many positive ways. I feel a much greater connection to nature and spirituality, and I am incredibly grateful for that.

No matter where you're at on your journey, hopefully, these recipes can help inspire you to introduce more plant-based meals into your life. Even better, here's hoping you love them as much as I do!

"Eating plants is not a sacrifice. It's a pleasure and a conscious choice
to honor your body, mind, and soul."

—**Michaela Vais** (@elavegan)

PANTRY ESSENTIALS

No matter your dietary requirements, having a well-stocked pantry is the key to kitchen success. Keeping a selection of basic ingredients on hand means fewer trips to the grocery store and the ability to pull together delicious meals at a moment's notice.

Not only are most of the ingredients I use easily accessible globally, but they're also budget-friendly and versatile in their uses. This trifecta helps to make vegan eating a breeze!

Legumes: Dried and canned chickpeas (garbanzo beans), white beans (cannellini, great northern, navy), kidney beans (red or white), pinto beans, black beans, lentils (red, green, and brown), peanuts

Plant-Based Milk: Almond milk, oat milk (or your favorite dairy-free milk like cashew milk, rice milk, soy milk, etc.), canned coconut milk

Condiments: Tomato sauce (passata), tomato paste, tamari or coconut aminos (or soy sauce if you consume gluten), balsamic vinegar, rice vinegar, apple cider vinegar, nutritional yeast, vegetable broth (regular and low sodium), mustard

Grains: Rice (white, brown, jasmine, basmati), pasta (regular, gluten-free, or grain-free) such as brown rice pasta, quinoa pasta, rice noodles, etc., quinoa (though it's technically a seed, not a grain), oats (quick and rolled)

Flours: Tapioca flour/starch, cornstarch, rice flour, chickpea flour (garbanzo bean flour/ gram flour), almond flour, coconut flour, oat flour, buckwheat flour, millet flour, all-purpose gluten-free flour

Nuts/Seeds: Cashews, almonds, walnuts, sunflower seeds, sesame seeds, pumpkin seeds (pepitas), shredded unsweetened coconut

Oils: Olive oil (extra virgin), coconut oil, sesame oil (regular and toasted), avocado oil

Spices: Salt (I use sea salt), black pepper, onion powder, garlic powder, paprika (sweet and smoked), oregano, thyme, rosemary, cumin, curry powder, turmeric, nutmeg, ginger, cinnamon, black salt (Kala Namak), cayenne powder (or chili powder), red pepper flakes

Herbs: Basil, bay leaves, cilantro (coriander), dill, parsley, rosemary, thyme

Egg Replacer: Flax seeds, chia seeds, psyllium husk powder, applesauce, aquafaba (chickpea brine), mashed bananas

Fresh Produce: Spinach, tomatoes (fresh and canned), broccoli, cauliflower, bell peppers, carrots, zucchini, cabbage, potatoes, sweet potatoes, cucumber, eggplant, mushrooms, pumpkin, lettuce, onions, garlic, ginger, berries, bananas, pineapple, apples, avocado, mango, lime, lemon, etc.

Dried Fruit: Raisins, dates (Medjool), apricots, cranberries

Superfoods: Cocoa powder (or cacao powder), hemp seeds, vegetable and fruit powders (beetroot, etc.)

Nut/Seed Butters: Peanut butter, cashew butter, almond butter, hazelnut butter, sunflower seed butter

Sweeteners: Coconut sugar, Erythritol, maple syrup, etc.

Tofu: Silken tofu, regular tofu (usually extra-firm)

For Baking: Dairy-free chocolate chips, baking powder, baking soda, vanilla extract (or vanilla paste)

INGREDIENT NOTES & SUBSTITUTIONS

One thing that you can rely on within this recipe book is plenty of ingredient substitutions to help you adapt recipes, if needed, to your kitchen and dietary requirements. Below are some of my most used ingredients, with notes on how I use them and their substitutions.

Legumes (Beans & Lentils): Not only are most legumes inexpensive (more so in dry form than tinned, though either work), but they're also super versatile and one of my primary sources of protein as a vegan. They're packed with plant-based protein, fiber, and various micronutrients and are perfect for creating filling and nutritious meat-free meals.

Whether mixing them into vegan meatloaf (page 157), blending them into a white bean dip (page 43), or even hiding them in oatmeal chocolate chip bars (page 213), there's no shortage of vegan recipes using legumes! You don't have to have them all on hand, either, though I recommend keeping two to three types available to mix and match in recipes.

Herbs, Spices, & Seasonings: These ingredients are the building blocks of all cooking, and I'm definitely not shy with seasonings in my recipes. Along with salt and pepper, herbs, spices, and seasonings take any recipe to the next level, adding complex flavors and depth. This is especially important when making healthy recipes with low fat, salt, and sugar levels.

If you want to save money, you can purchase inexpensive spices and seasonings from Asian and Middle Eastern markets. Just note that dried spices are best when used within six months and lose their potency after that. You can also grow fresh herbs (basil, mint, rosemary, etc.) to save money in the long run.

While a spice cupboard can quickly overflow with all the options out there, in my cooking, I've found there is a variety of options that I return to repeatedly (see page 17).

Flour: All of my recipes are gluten-free, which means I always have a selection of flours on hand to choose from. However, most of the time, you can use regular all-purpose flour or spelt flour if a recipe calls for rice flour or all-purpose GF (gluten-free) flour. It's much easier to replace gluten-free flour than to replace regular flour. Also, please note that gluten-free baked goods are often not as fluffy as wheat-based baked goods and won't rise as much because of the lack of gluten. Luckily, you can still achieve satisfying results by using baking powder and baking soda.

Starches: There are several starches that I keep stocked in my pantry, including cornstarch, tapioca flour/starch, arrowroot flour, and potato starch. In many cases, they can be used interchangeably, though some uses are unique to specific starches. For example, tapioca flour (tapioca starch) thickens sauces and is great for gluten-free baking. However, it also has stretchy, "gummy" properties, perfect for vegan cheese recipes like my easy vegan cheese sauce (page 31).

As a substitute, I often turn to arrowroot flour for its similar properties. In comparison, I use cornstarch and potato starch in place of flour to thicken sauces (that don't require stretchiness) or soups.

Oat Flour: Many of my desserts contain oat flour (finely ground oats), and while you can purchase it, I prefer to make my own. You can grind the oats in a blender or electric coffee/spice grinder to make your own oat flour in seconds. Unfortunately, while oats are naturally gluten-free, they are often processed in facilities with the risk of cross-contamination. For that reason, if you are celiac, use certified gluten-free oats. Many times, it's possible to use **buckwheat flour** (also naturally gluten-free) instead of oat flour, and **millet flakes** instead of quick oats.

Almond Flour: It's simply 100 percent ground blanched almonds and is available in several levels of coarseness (ranging from coarse almond meal to superfine almond flour). You can make almond flour by pulsing blanched almonds in a blender or electric coffee/spice grinder, though it won't be as fine as "superfine" store-bought versions.

Almond flour contains healthy fats, fiber, proteins, vitamin E, and magnesium and adds a delicious, subtle nutty flavor and moisture to baked goods, perfect for vegan and gluten-free baking (pages 63, 64, 71, 75–79, 84, 211–241). If a recipe calls for almond flour, you can often substitute other ground nuts *or* seeds (e.g., sunflower seeds) instead.

Coconut Flour: It's very high in fiber, has unique properties, and is popular in keto recipes for its low-carb macros. However, I only use it in a few recipes (e.g., peanut butter truffles on page 222) because it's very absorbent and requires further recipe tweaks. Please do *not* use coconut flour if a recipe calls for any other flours or shredded unsweetened coconut, as it's not easily interchangeable.

Egg Substitute: "Flax eggs" or "chia eggs" are popular vegan egg replacements. One tablespoon of ground flaxseed (or ground chia seeds) mixed with three tablespoons of water left to rest and thicken for five minutes will replace one regular egg. However, they work best in recipes that only require one or two "eggs," like my healthy peanut butter cookies (page 225).

Alternatively, you can use applesauce, mashed banana, or aquafaba as vegan egg replacements.

Aquafaba: Aquafaba refers to the brine in a can of chickpeas (or the leftover cooking water from cooking dried chickpeas). This miracle liquid mimics egg whites beautifully and will whip into stiff peaks without imparting a strong flavor or color. As a result, it's a great egg white alternative in many dishes, including vegan meringues, marshmallows, and mousses (page 237).

Psyllium Husk: Psyllium is a soluble fiber that supports digestive health. It's a wonderful ingredient for gluten-free baking as it acts similar to gluten. I use it in my popular gluten-free bread recipe (page 59), resulting in a loaf that looks and feels almost like regular wheat bread from a bakery! You can also use it in smaller quantities to replace eggs.

Nutritional Yeast: This is a must-have in my vegan kitchen. Made from deactivated yeast (often fortified with B-vitamins), its cheesy, slightly nutty, umami flavor makes it perfect for making vegan cheese and adding depth to dishes. I love using it for vegan cheese sauce (page 31) or sprinkling it over pasta, potatoes, or rice. I also use it to make homemade crackers (page 184). You could alternatively use miso paste or shiitake mushroom powder as an umami-rich replacement, though it won't provide a cheesy flavor.

Agar Powder: It's a wonderful, all-natural, algae-based vegan substitution for gelatin, used to help vegan no-bake cheesecakes (page 233) or vegan cheeses/mozzarella (page 51) set to the correct consistency.

Plant-Based Milk: I live in the tropics and often use unsweetened canned coconut milk (or homemade coconut milk). It's thick, creamy, and perfect for curries (pages 133-134, 158 etc.) or desserts that don't contain oil, thanks to its higher fat content.

If a recipe calls specifically for canned coconut milk, I usually don't recommend replacing it with boxed dairy-free milk (which is far thinner and contains less fat) unless you add extra oil to the recipe to compensate for the missing fat content. Refer to specific recipes for more details.

Sugar: I avoid refined sugar, preferring to rely on unprocessed and natural sweeteners. Along with dates, I like to use coconut sugar. I also include options for sugar alternatives in many of my recipes, such as Erythritol, a popular keto sugar alternative great for diabetics and those reducing their sugar intake.

If you aren't watching your sugar intake, you can always use regular (organic) white sugar, cane sugar, or brown sugar.

Maple syrup: Pure maple syrup is my number one liquid sweetener. It's refined, sugar-free, and has a rich flavor that works perfectly in many of my recipes, like strawberry crumb bars (page 75) and banana baked oatmeal (page 63). However, in most cases, it's okay to substitute maple syrup with any other liquid sweetener (e.g., rice malt syrup, date syrup, agave syrup [not refined sugar-free], etc.).

If preferred, you can also experiment with sugar-free syrups (like keto maple syrup). Refer to individual recipes for more information, though, as sometimes the sugar is required in a recipe for more than just flavor.

Silken Tofu: With a wonderful silky texture, this is packed with protein, low fat, even more neutral in taste compared to regular tofu. I mainly use it in vegan cheesecakes (page 233), but you could substitute soy-free vegan cream cheese (e.g., almond cream cheese).

Cashew Nuts: Cashews are one of my favorite pantry staples. They contain lots of vitamins and minerals and are almost unbelievably versatile, thanks to their subtle flavor and creamy consistency. They are loved by many vegans because once soaked and blended into a cream, you can use them to make creamy sauces, vegan mozzarella (page 51), vegan cheesecakes (page 233), and plenty of other desserts and dishes.

I recommend soaking cashews overnight in cold water or for at least an hour in hot water, or boiling them for 20 minutes. Not only are they better digested this way (like all nuts), but they will also blend easier and smoother. For a nut-free substitution, use hulled hemp seeds or soaked sunflower seeds.

Oils: I try to use oils sparingly but keep a few on hand for different uses. For example, I enjoy using coconut oil for frying (though it has a subtle coconut flavor). Avocado oil is great too and has a high smoke point and neutral flavor. Sesame oil (regular and toasted) is great for Asian-style cooking. I also often use extra virgin olive oil, usually in salad dressings (pages 108, 112, 115) and other no or low-heat recipes.

EQUIPMENT

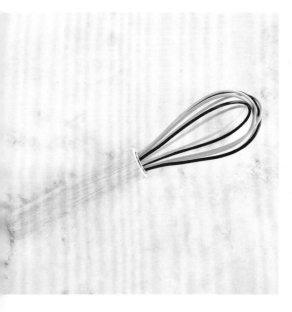

New "must-have" kitchen gadgets and tools are always coming onto the market. However, as anyone with cupboards and drawers filled with unused items knows, many of them aren't worth the purchase. You don't need to fill every kitchen surface to be a successful home cook. Relying on just a few tried-and-tested tools and gadgets is more than enough. Here are the ones I return to repeatedly and are all you need to create every single recipe in this book.

Kitchen Scale: All my recipes use both metric and cup measurements, but metric measurements are far more precise, especially for gluten-free, vegan baking. I recommend using a kitchen scale for precise and accurate results!

Food Processor: I love my food processor and use it almost daily! It's super versatile and great for cutting back on prep time. For example, it's great for chopping and shredding vegetables quickly, as well as making a cake crust—perfect for no-bake cake recipes (pages 233, 241), mixing dough, blending nut butter and hummus (page 40), and more! If you don't have one yet, get one. They're very affordable and super practical.

Blender: I use it for my desserts (pages 211-241), sauces (pages 31-47), and soups (pages 119-141). If you want a smoother result, a blender performs better than a food processor. You don't need a super-expensive high-speed blender that costs an arm and a leg, either! Some cheaper blenders that cost $100 are often more than enough for everyday use. My secret is to blend long enough until everything is smooth and creamy, giving the machine breaks in between.

Immersion Blender: Blending soups can be a bit of a dangerous and messy game when trying to use a regular blender. Luckily, an immersion blender can go directly into your soup pot, and voila! Immersion blenders are also great for dressings, sauces, and other "low volume" blending needs. As a bonus, they take up little space and are easy to clean.

Air Fryer: My air fryer allows me to cook super crisp and delicious foods with minimal oil while speeding up the cooking process. While it's not exactly small, it's invaluable and I use it every other day for crispy falafels (page 188), fries, nuggets, and more!

Electric Spice/Coffee Grinder: Perhaps surprisingly, I don't use these grinders very often for their intended purpose (though they work excellently for grinding whole peppercorns and cumin seeds). Instead, I find them great for grinding small quantities of nuts, seeds, pulses, and oats into flour.

Hand Mixer: While I don't use it too often, this tool saves time and arm power when whipping up batters and aquafaba (for example, with vegan mousse—page 237).

Springform Pans: I use different-sized springform pans. They are 4 inches (10 cm) for mini cakes, 6 inches (15 cm), or 8 inches (20 cm) in diameter. Springform pans have a removable bottom/sides, making it easier to unmold cakes, tarts, and more.

Muffin Pan: I love making muffins, like chocolate muffins (page 76), and use a muffin pan regularly. I recommend a metal or silicone pan. Please note that muffins baked in a silicone pan often require a longer baking time.

Nonstick Oven Trays: While nonstick isn't necessary, it can help with clean-up. Lining your baking trays with parchment paper or a Silpat sheet is also great for easy clean-up and helps make the trays last longer. You'll need at least a couple of large baking sheets/oven trays.

Skillet: I recommend owning at least one good quality nonstick skillet/pan. Not only does nonstick mean less oil, but it makes it easy to care for, too. I also have a **Cast Iron Pan**, but it's more difficult to make items like gluten-free tortillas or wraps (pages 52 and 56) in them, and they require more care and upkeep. I recommend having a selection of skillets and saucepans in different sizes (at least one medium and one large skillet and a small, medium, and large saucepan).

Small Tools: Along with my main gadgets, there are several pieces of smaller kitchenware that I think no kitchen should be without, including:

- Vegetable peeler & grater
- Measuring spoons & cups
- Whisk
- Tongs
- Assorted wooden and silicone spoons and spatulas
- Silicone pastry brush (not used often, but very handy when needed)
- A selection of mixing bowls in different sizes
- Sharp knives (paring, utility, and chef)
- Cutting boards
- Fine mesh strainer and colander
- Nut milk bag
- Reusable silicone zip-top bags and airtight glass containers and jars (to store leftovers)

BASICS, SAUCES, & DIPS

VEGAN CHEESE SAUCE

5 minutes, 3 servings

¾ cup (180 ml/6.3 oz) canned
   coconut milk (see notes)

3 Tbsp (20 g/0.7 oz) nutritional yeast

2 Tbsp (15 g/0.5 oz) tapioca flour/
   starch (see notes)

½ tsp salt (or to taste)

½ tsp onion powder (optional)

¼ tsp garlic powder (optional)

1 pinch of smoked paprika (optional)

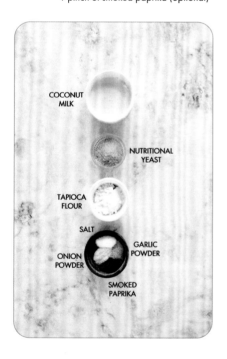

Instructions

1. Add all the ingredients to a saucepan and whisk well. Once everything is combined, turn on the heat and bring the mixture to a boil, stirring constantly.

2. Let it simmer on low to medium heat for about 1 minute until the sauce is stretchy and thickened.

3. Enjoy this vegan cheese sauce with nachos, on pizza (pages 55, 203), over pasta, and on many other savory dishes!

Notes

- **Thickness:** If the cheese sauce turns out too thick, add more coconut milk or any other plant-based milk (or water), up to 1 cup. If it's too thin, add more starch (combined with a liquid to avoid lumps).

- **Coconut milk:** I use canned coconut milk that contains 17 percent fat. If you don't like the taste of coconut milk, use a different plant-based milk instead (e.g., almond milk, cashew milk, etc.). The higher the fat content of the milk, the creamier the vegan cheese sauce will be.

- **Tapioca substitute:** Arrowroot flour (also known as arrowroot powder or arrowroot starch) is a great substitute for tapioca flour/starch.

CHINESE GARLIC SAUCE

10 minutes, 4 servings

SAUCE

½ cup (120 ml/4.2 oz)
   vegetable broth

3 Tbsp low-sodium GF soy sauce
   (see notes)

2 Tbsp rice vinegar

2 Tbsp maple syrup (see notes)

½ tsp sesame oil

¼ tsp red pepper flakes
   (or less/more to taste)

¼ tsp smoked paprika

1 Tbsp cornstarch (see notes)

½ tsp Szechuan peppercorns
   (optional)

2 tsp Chinese rice wine or dry sherry
   (optional)

PAN

½ Tbsp vegetable oil (see notes)

4 tsp fresh garlic, minced
   (4 garlic cloves)

2 tsp fresh ginger, minced

Instructions

1. Add all sauce ingredients to a medium-sized bowl and whisk, then set aside.

2. Next, heat the vegetable oil in a saucepan or skillet over medium heat. Add the fresh garlic and ginger and sauté for 30–60 seconds, stirring frequently.

3. Whisk the sauce again, then pour it into the saucepan. Bring to a boil and simmer for a few minutes until thickened, stirring frequently.

4. Use the sauce immediately, for example, in a stir-fry or as a dip for dumplings. Or let it cool completely and pour the sauce into a clean jar. Enjoy!

Notes

*   **Vegetable oil:** Use canola oil, vegetable cooking oil, or any neutral cooking oil. For an oil-free version, use more vegetable broth instead.

*   **Sweetener:** I use maple syrup. However, any other sweetener is fine.

*   **Cornstarch:** You can use arrowroot flour, tapioca flour/starch, or potato starch.

*   **Soy sauce:** Use a combination of light and dark soy sauces for extra depth of flavor. Use tamari or gluten-free soy sauce if you have a gluten allergy. If you want a soy-free alternative, use coconut aminos.

*   Store leftovers covered in the fridge for between 4 and 5 days.

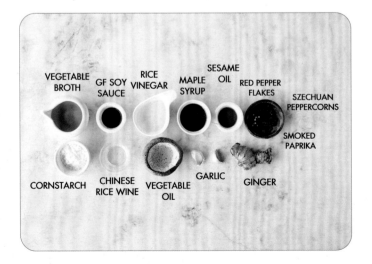

FLAVORFUL MUSHROOM GRAVY

20 minutes, 7 servings

28 g (1 oz) dried mushrooms (e.g., porcini, white button, chanterelle)

2 ¾ cups (650 ml/22.9 oz) vegetable broth

1 Tbsp oil or water

1 onion, diced

3 garlic cloves, minced

¾ tsp fresh thyme

1 ½ tsp fresh rosemary

Salt and black pepper to taste

⅓ cup (80 ml/2.8 oz) plant-based milk

4 Tbsp (32 g/1.1 oz) cornstarch (or arrowroot flour)

1 Tbsp GF soy sauce, tamari, or coconut aminos

¼ cup (60 ml/2.1 oz) red wine (optional)

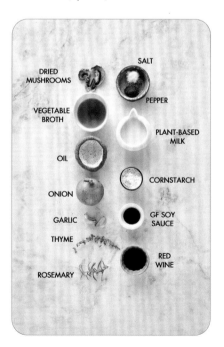

Instructions

1. Add the dried mushrooms to a medium saucepan and pour in the vegetable broth. Bring it to a boil over high heat and cook for about 1 minute, then turn off the heat and set aside.

2. Heat oil in a large skillet or pot over medium heat, add the onion, and sauté for 2–3 minutes. Add garlic, thyme, rosemary, salt, and black pepper, and sauté for 1 minute, stirring frequently.

3. Meanwhile, combine plant-based milk and cornstarch in a small bowl. Whisk until it's lump-free, then set aside.

4. Add the soy sauce and red wine (optional) to the skillet while stirring.

5. Next, add the rehydrated mushrooms with the broth to the cornstarch mixture and stir to combine. Let the gravy simmer and thicken for about 5 minutes, or longer if you want it to be even more flavorful and thick.

6. I use an immersion blender to blend the gravy. However, you can also transfer the gravy to a blender and blend until smooth. If the gravy is too thick, add more vegetable broth. If it's too thin, add more cornstarch/arrowroot flour.

7. Taste and adjust the seasonings. Reheat the gravy in a pan/skillet and serve over mashed potatoes (page 107), vegan meatloaf (page 157), potato dumplings (page 104), etc.

8. Store any leftovers covered in the fridge for 4 days or in the freezer for 2 months.

CREAMY PEANUT SAUCE

5 minutes, 9 servings

⅓ cup (80 g/2.8 oz) creamy peanut
    butter (see notes)

2 Tbsp GF soy sauce, tamari, or
    coconut aminos

1½ Tbsp rice vinegar or lime juice

1½ Tbsp coconut sugar (see notes)

1 pinch of red pepper flakes (optional)

½ tsp cumin powder (optional)

½ Tbsp fresh ginger, grated

2 small garlic cloves, grated

2–3 Tbsp dairy-free milk or water,
    to thin

PEANUT BUTTER

GF SOY SAUCE

RICE VINEGAR

GROUND CUMIN

COCONUT SUGAR

RED PEPPER FLAKES

GINGER

GARLIC

DAIRY-FREE MILK

Instructions

1. I recommend heating the peanut butter in a double boiler (or microwave) until softened. Then, mix all the ingredients, except the dairy-free milk (or water), in a bowl with a whisk *(or use an immersion blender)*.

2. Slowly stir in the milk/water, 1 tablespoon at a time, to thin the sauce. Use more milk/water for a peanut dressing for salads.

3. Taste the sauce and add more rice vinegar/lime juice, sweetener, and/or soy sauce, if needed.

Notes

- **Peanut butter:** You can also use sunflower seed butter.

- **Sweetener:** For this recipe I used coconut sugar, but you can use any other sweetener.

- Store leftovers in the fridge in a glass jar for up to 1 week.

AVOCADO BASIL PESTO

5 minutes, 11 servings

1 medium (200 g/7.1 oz) avocado
(weight without core and shell)

1 cup (20 g/0.7 oz) fresh basil

⅓ cup (45 g/1.6 oz) hemp seeds

1 tsp nutritional yeast (optional)

½ tsp salt

¼ tsp black pepper

3 garlic cloves

2 Tbsp lemon juice or lime juice

1 ½ Tbsp olive oil (optional, see notes)

Instructions

1. Add all ingredients to a food processor and blend for about 20–30 seconds.

2. Transfer the pesto into a glass jar.

3. Enjoy it with pasta, over bread (page 59), pizza (pages 55, 203), and more!

Notes

- **For oil-free pesto:** Thanks to the creaminess of the avocado, you can get away with omitting the oil. However, a little will provide the silky mouthfeel and subtle flavor.

- Store it in the fridge for 3–4 days or in the freezer for 3 months.

AVOCADO

FRESH BASIL

HEMP SEEDS

NUTRITIONAL YEAST

PEPPER

SALT

GARLIC

LEMON JUICE

OLIVE OIL

CREAMY HUMMUS

25 minutes, 4–6 servings

1 can (425 g/15 oz) chickpeas

⅓ tsp baking soda

4 Tbsp (40 ml/1.4 oz) lemon juice
  (or more to taste)

2–3 small garlic cloves

⅓ tsp salt (or more to taste)

¼ tsp ground cumin

4 Tbsp (40 ml/1.4 oz)
  plant-based milk (or more for
  a creamier hummus)

¼ cup (60 g/2.1 oz) creamy tahini

Olive oil to drizzle (optional)

Paprika for garnish

Fresh parsley for garnish

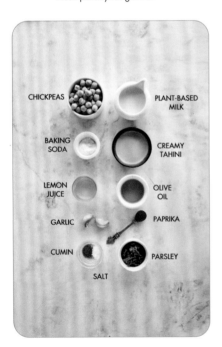

Instructions

1. Rinse and drain the canned chickpeas and transfer them to a medium saucepan with ⅓ tsp baking soda. Cover them with at least 2 inches (ca. 5 cm) of water and bring to a boil over high heat.

2. Boil the chickpeas for about 15 minutes until very tender and slightly mushy, then drain them in a strainer, rinse with cool water, and set aside.

3. Process the lemon juice, garlic, salt, cumin, half the plant-based milk, and tahini in a food processor until smooth. Pause the food processor to scrape down the sides.

4. Add the chickpeas and blend for a further 1–2 minutes, scraping down the sides of the processor as needed.

5. Next, add the remaining plant-based milk and blend for 1–2 minutes until smooth, creamy, and fluffy.

6. Taste the hummus and add more salt and/or lemon juice accordingly.

7. Serve in a bowl and top with more lemon juice, olive oil, a pinch of paprika (or smoked paprika), and fresh parsley.

Notes

- Store leftovers covered in the fridge for up to 4 days.

WHITE BEAN DIP

35 minutes, 4 servings

ROASTED VEGGIES

1 small garlic head

1 cup (180 g/6.3 oz) cherry tomatoes

1 sweet pepper sliced (color of choice)

1 ½ Tbsp olive oil

2 pinches of salt

WHITE BEAN DIP

1 can (425 g/15 oz) white beans,
    drained and rinsed

⅓ tsp salt

½ tsp onion powder

2 tsp nutritional yeast

½ tsp Italian seasoning

Black pepper to taste

1 ½ Tbsp (24 g/0.8 oz) tahini or
    cashew butter

1 ½ Tbsp lemon juice

6–8 Tbsp water to thin

Parsley for garnish (optional)

Instructions

1. Preheat the oven to 400°F (205°C), then cut off the top of the head of garlic (about ¼–½ inch resp. 0.6–1.2 cm).

2. Add the cherry tomatoes, pepper, and garlic to a baking dish, drizzle with oil, and season with salt. Cover the garlic with a ramekin (or tin foil) and roast for about 30 minutes.

3. Let the garlic cool until you can handle it, then gently squeeze the garlic cloves from the head straight into the blender. Add the remaining dip ingredients (not the roasted veggies) and blend until completely smooth. Use enough water to blend, starting with a few tablespoons and increasing as needed.

4. Transfer the mixture to a shallow bowl and create a swirl with the back of a spoon.

5. Top with the roasted vegetables (along with the remaining oil from the baking dish). Sprinkle with fresh parsley and optional chili powder. Enjoy with naan or pita!

Notes

*   **Adjust the thickness:** Alter the amount of added water in the dip/spread.

*   **Adjust to taste:** Adjust the amount of tahini, lemon juice, garlic, and any of the seasonings to taste (start by adding less than called for and increase to your liking).

*   **To save time:** You can lightly sauté the garlic and the veggies for the topping for a few minutes instead of roasting them (adjust the garlic amount accordingly).

*   Store leftovers covered in the fridge for up to 4 days.

CHOCOLATE SPREAD

5 minutes, 10 servings

¼ cup (70 g/2.5 oz) hazelnut butter
   (see notes)

4 Tbsp (80 g/2.8 oz) maple syrup or
   liquid sweetener of choice

3 Tbsp (18 g/0.6 oz) cocoa powder,
   unsweetened

2 Tbsp water or plant-based milk

1 tsp vanilla extract

1 pinch of salt

1 pinch of instant coffee (optional)

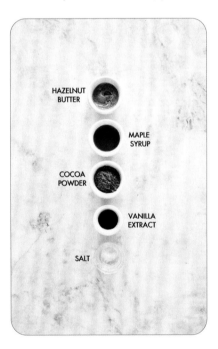

HAZELNUT
BUTTER

MAPLE
SYRUP

COCOA
POWDER

VANILLA
EXTRACT

SALT

Instructions

1. Add all the ingredients to a medium-sized bowl and whisk until smooth and creamy.

2. Taste it and add more maple syrup if you want it sweeter! Add more nut butter and cocoa powder for a thicker cream or more water for a thinner chocolate spread. Enjoy as a bread spread or as a brownie glaze (pages 230, 241).

Notes

*   **Hazelnut butter:** You can use another nut butter (peanut, almond, etc.), or use sunflower seed butter for a nut-free version.

*   You can melt **dairy-free chocolate chips** and add a few tablespoons for an ultra-rich spread!

*   Add a tiny pinch of **instant coffee** (or room temperature espresso liquid instead of the water) to enhance the chocolate flavor.

*   Store leftovers covered in an airtight container in the fridge for up to 1 week.

RASPBERRY JAM

15 minutes, 14 servings

1 ½ cups (200 g/7.1 oz)
    raspberries, frozen

2 Tbsp (20 g/0.7 oz) chia seeds

2–3 Tbsp (40–60 g/1.4–2.1 oz)
    maple syrup or to taste (see notes)

1 tsp fresh lemon juice or lime juice
    (more to taste)

½ tsp vanilla extract

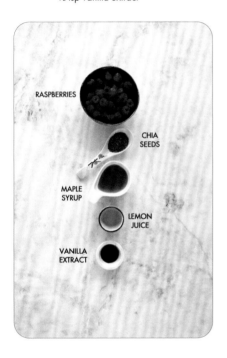

RASPBERRIES

CHIA
SEEDS

MAPLE
SYRUP

LEMON
JUICE

VANILLA
EXTRACT

Instructions

1. Add the frozen raspberries to a saucepan or skillet and bring them to a low simmer. Stir with a wooden spoon or spatula, pressing and crushing them until they break down into tiny pieces.

2. Remove the saucepan from the heat and stir in all the remaining ingredients. Use less maple syrup first, taste the mixture and add more if needed.

3. Let the jam cool for a bit, then transfer it to a clean glass jar and store it in the fridge (for up to 5 days), where it will thicken further within a few hours.

4. Enjoy on toast, banana bread, in cookies (page 229), etc.

Notes

*   **Maple syrup:** You can use any other sweetener like date syrup, brown rice syrup, etc. Use a keto sweetener (like Erythritol) for a low-carb jam.

*   **Berries:** I used thawed raspberries that were very juicy for this recipe. If you use fresh raspberries, you might need to add a little water.

QUICK OAT MILK

5 minutes, 9 servings

1 cup (90 g/3.2 oz) ground oats
  (oat flour—see notes)

4 cups (960 ml/33.9 oz) water
  (see notes)

1–2 pitted dates (see notes)

1 tsp vanilla extract

2 pinches of salt

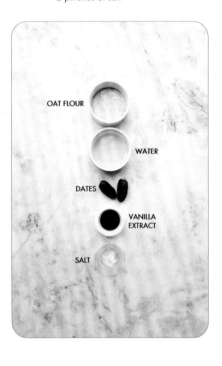

Instructions

1. Add all the ingredients to a high-speed blender and blend for 10 seconds. If using a less powerful blender, I recommend blending all the ingredients except the oat flour first (for about 30–40 seconds), then adding the oat flour and blending for just 10 seconds. *The longer you blend, the slimier the oat milk becomes.*

2. Strain the milk through a nut milk bag.

3. Transfer it to a sealable container like a glass bottle for 3–4 days in the fridge, or enjoy it immediately with granola, milkshakes, etc.

Notes

- **Make your own oat flour** by blending rolled oats (regular or gluten-free) in a blender or electric coffee/spice grinder. Alternatively, you can use plain oats, but the oat milk turns out better with ground oats.

- I use **Medjool dates**, but you can use other dates as well. Use 1–2, depending on how sweet you prefer it.

- **Don't use warm or hot water:** It will lead to slimy oat milk, as it will activate the enzyme in oats that causes them to thicken.

- **Optional add-ins:** Adding 3–4 tablespoons of almond flour (or any nut/seed flour, like cashews, sunflower seeds, etc.) will make the milk richer and creamier.

VEGAN MOZZARELLA

25 minutes, 6 servings

½ cup (75 g/2.6 oz) cashews

1 small potato, peeled and chopped

1 cup (240 ml/8.5 oz) dairy-free
    milk (see notes)

4 Tbsp (30 g/1.1 oz) tapioca flour/
    starch (see notes)

1 Tbsp nutritional yeast

2 tsp white vinegar or lemon juice

¾ tsp salt

¼ tsp onion powder

For Firm Mozzarella

2 Tbsp agar powder optional
    (see notes)

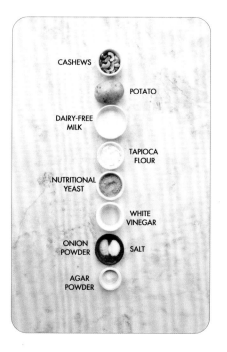

CASHEWS

POTATO

DAIRY-FREE
MILK

TAPIOCA
FLOUR

NUTRITIONAL
YEAST

WHITE
VINEGAR

ONION
POWDER   SALT

AGAR
POWDER

Instructions

1. Soak the cashews in hot water for an hour or boil them for 10–15 minutes. Then, discard the water.

2. Meanwhile, boil the potato in a saucepan filled with salted water until it's tender, then drain the water. You will need 80 grams of cooked potato (⅓ of a cup mashed with a fork). It's also possible to boil the cashews and potato together!

3. Add all the ingredients to a blender and blend until super smooth.

4. Pour the mixture into a saucepan and bring it to a boil. Reduce the heat and let it simmer for a few minutes until thick and stretchy, then turn off the heat.

5. It's best to use it immediately, for example, on pizza (pages 55, 203) or toast. You can also transfer it to a bowl and store it covered in the fridge for 2–3 days, though the texture will change (it will become softer and creamy after a while, like cream cheese). Enjoy!

Notes

*   **Firm cheese:** If you want to make firm (sliceable) vegan mozzarella, add either 1 ½ Tbsp kappa carrageenan or 2 Tbsp of agar powder (100 percent strength) and cook the cheese mixture for at least 5–6 minutes (please note it will be very thick, so stirring often is essential). Pour the mixture into an oiled/greased bowl and let it chill for a couple of hours (preferably in the fridge) until firm. Kappa carrageenan will make the cheese firmer than agar powder.

*   **Milk:** I use canned coconut milk (17 percent fat) since it's super creamy (I use it in my vegan cheese sauce on page 31 too), but you can use another milk or even water.

*   **Tapioca:** I recommend tapioca starch as it makes the mozzarella stretchy. You might be able to substitute arrowroot flour, though, but the result won't be as good.

GLUTEN-FREE TORTILLAS/WRAPS

15 minutes, 4 servings

1 heaped cup (120 g/4.2 oz) chickpea
    flour (garbanzo bean flour)
½ cup (60 g/2.1 oz) tapioca flour/
    starch (see notes)
1 cup (240 ml/8.5 oz) water
⅓ tsp salt
Oil to fry

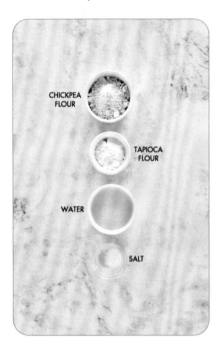

Instructions

1. Process the ingredients in your food processor (or whisk them together in a bowl) into a batter. Use more water for thin wraps/crêpes. Use less than 1 cup of water for thicker tortillas for tacos (pages 195, 204).

2. Heat a little oil in a nonstick pan/skillet over medium heat. Pour about ⅓ cup of the batter into the pan/skillet (⅓ cup is a good size for a taco) or use more batter if you want to make enchiladas.

3. Cook for 2 minutes over low-medium heat, flip the tortilla, and cook for about one minute. Enjoy!

Notes

- **Tapioca flour/starch:** You can use arrowroot flour instead of tapioca flour/starch.

- **Storage:** Let the tortillas cool entirely. I recommend stacking them on a plate and putting some wax paper between the wraps, so they don't stick together. You can store them in the fridge for up to 3 days, wrapped in plastic wrap. They dry out a bit in the fridge, but you can reheat them individually in a pan (on both sides over low/medium heat for about 30 seconds) until soft and elastic/pliable again. It's also possible to freeze them for up to 3 months!

GLUTEN-FREE PIZZA CRUST

70 minutes, 6–8 servings

YEAST MIXTURE

¾ cup + 2 Tbsp (200 ml/7.1 oz)
  warm plant-based milk

1½ tsp active dry yeast

1 tsp olive oil

½ Tbsp (10 g/0.4 oz) maple syrup or
  agave syrup

DRY INGREDIENTS

1 cup (160 g/5.6 oz) white rice flour

½ cup (60 g/2.1 oz) tapioca flour/
  starch

⅓ cup (40 g/1.4 oz) cornstarch or
  potato starch

2 tsp psyllium husk powder

⅓ tsp salt

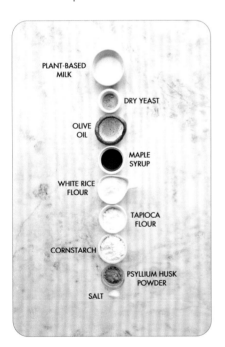

Instructions

1. Heat the plant-based milk in a saucepan for a few seconds until it's lukewarm (not hot!), about 35–40°C (95–104°F). Add all the other ingredients for the yeast mixture and set aside for 5–10 minutes to activate the yeast. If it starts to get frothy, then the yeast is active.

2. Combine all the dry ingredients in a bowl and stir with a whisk.

3. Add the yeast mixture and stir with a wooden spoon. The dough might seem too wet at first, but that will change within a minute.

4. Knead the dough with your hands for a few minutes, then form a dough ball and place it back in the bowl. Cover the bowl with a clean damp kitchen towel and set aside (in a warm place) for about 30–60 minutes until it's risen.

5. Next, preheat the oven to 390°F (200°C).

6. Place the dough onto a parchment-lined/greased baking tray and use your fingers to spread it into your preferred pizza shape. Allow it to rest for 10 minutes, preparing all the toppings in the meantime.

7. Top with tomato sauce (and other toppings of choice), then bake in the oven for 10–15 minutes. Add dollops of vegan mozzarella (page 51) on the pizza and bake for another 10–15 minutes (or until golden and crispy). Cut the pizza into 6–8 pieces, optionally top with fresh basil, and enjoy!

GLUTEN-FREE SPINACH TORTILLAS/WRAPS

20 minutes, 6–7 wraps

1 heaped cup (120 g/4.2 oz) chickpea
  flour (garbanzo bean flour)

½ cup (60 g/2.1 oz) tapioca flour/
  starch or arrowroot flour

2 cups (60 g/2.1 oz) fresh baby
  spinach leaves

1⅛ cup (270 ml/9.5 oz) water

⅓ tsp salt

Oil to fry

Instructions

1. Process all the ingredients in your food processor or blender until the batter is smooth. Use a little more water if you want to make thinner/bigger wraps (page 52).

2. Heat a little oil in a nonstick pan/skillet over medium heat. Pour about ⅓ cup of the batter into the pan/skillet.

3. Cook for 2 minutes over medium-low heat, flip the tortilla, and cook on the other side for about 1 minute. Enjoy!

GLUTEN-FREE BREAD

85 minutes, 12 servings/slices

PSYLLIUM MIXTURE

1¾ cup (420 ml / 14.8 oz) water

2 Tbsp (30 ml / 1.1 oz) apple cider
vinegar (or lemon juice)

3½ Tbsp (30 g / 1.1 oz) psyllium husk
powder (see notes)

DRY INGREDIENTS

¾ cup + 1 Tbsp (100 g / 3.5 oz)
buckwheat flour

⅔ cup (100 g / 3.5 oz) white rice flour

1 cup (100 g / 3.5 oz) chickpea flour

5 Tbsp (40 g / 1.4 oz) tapioca flour/
starch (see notes)

1 tsp baking powder

½ tsp baking soda

1 tsp salt

⅜ cup (50 g / 1.8 oz) pumpkin seeds

Instructions

1. I recommend using metric measurements. In a bowl, combine the water and apple cider vinegar with the psyllium husk powder and whisk well. It will gel instantly and become thick. Set aside for 20–30 minutes.

2. Meanwhile, measure/weigh all the dry ingredients and add them to a large bowl. Preheat the oven to 390°F (200°C).

3. Add the psyllium gel to the bowl and knead the ingredients with a hand/stand mixer (use a dough hook). You can also knead the dough with your hands. It will take about 5–10 minutes for the dough to come together.

4. If the dough appears too wet, sprinkle it with 1–2 Tbsp tapioca flour. If it feels too dry, add a little water.

5. Shape the dough into a round or rectangular loaf and place it on a baking sheet lined with parchment paper (I sprinkled the paper with a bit of tapioca flour).

6. Bake for 50–60 minutes. Let the bread cool completely, then slice and enjoy.

Notes

- **Psyllium husk powder** is the most important ingredient in this recipe and cannot be substituted. If you only have whole psyllium husk, blend it in a blender or electric spice/coffee grinder into a fine powder.

- **Tapioca:** You can use arrowroot flour instead of tapioca flour/starch. Cornstarch or potato starch will most likely work as well.

- Store leftovers covered in the fridge for up to 6 days or in the freezer for up to 3 months!

BREAKFASTS

BANANA BAKED OATMEAL

45 minutes, 6 servings

2 small (140 g/4.9 oz) ripe bananas (weight without peel) (see notes)

3 Tbsp (50 g/1.8 oz) creamy peanut butter (see notes)

2 Tbsp (40 g/1.4 oz) maple syrup or any other liquid sweetener

1 tsp vanilla extract

1 ½ cups (360 ml/12.7 oz) plant-based milk of choice

1 ½ Tbsp ground chia seeds or flax seeds

¾ tsp ground cinnamon

⅛ tsp each of cardamom, nutmeg, and ground cloves

1 tsp baking powder

¼ tsp salt

2 cups (180 g/6.3 oz) quick oats, gluten-free if needed (see notes)

¼ cup nuts or seeds of choice (see notes)

Instructions

1. Preheat the oven to 350°F (177°C) and grease a 6x9 inch (15x23 cm) or similar-sized baking pan with oil.

2. In a large bowl, mash the 2 bananas with a fork. Add in peanut butter, maple syrup, and vanilla extract. Mix until well combined.

3. Pour in the plant-based milk gradually while whisking. Then, add the chia seeds and whisk again.

4. Stir in the spices, baking powder, and salt. Also, add the oats in batches, stirring with a spatula. You can now also add the chopped nuts or seeds.

5. Pour the mixture into the prepared pan and optionally top the oatmeal with 2 additional thinly sliced bananas. Bake for 35–40 minutes (depending on the size of the pan) or until the oatmeal is set and golden brown.

6. Remove it from the oven and let it cool for a couple of minutes. Serve warm, drizzle with peanut butter and/or maple syrup, and top with chopped nuts if you like. Enjoy!

Notes

- **Bananas:** You could use pumpkin purée instead of bananas.

- **Peanut butter:** You can use almond butter or any other nut butter (or even sunflower seed butter).

- **Oats:** I use quick oats, but rolled oats should work fine too.

- **Nuts:** You can use walnuts, pecans, almonds, cashews, etc. Use pumpkin seeds or any other seeds for a nut-free version.

- Store leftovers covered in the fridge for up to 5 days or in the freezer for up to 2 months. Reheat in the oven or microwave.

BANANA OAT PANCAKES

20 minutes, 5 pancakes

1 cup (90 g/3.2 oz) oat flour
  (gluten-free if needed) (see notes)

⅔ cup (160 ml/5.6 oz) lite coconut
  milk (canned) (see notes)

½ (65 g/2.3 oz) banana
  (weight without peel) (see notes)

OPTIONAL INGREDIENTS

1–2 Tbsp maple syrup for sweeter
  pancakes

¾ tsp baking powder for fluffier
  pancakes

1 pinch of salt

BANANA

OAT
FLOUR

COCONUT
MILK

MAPLE
SYRUP

SALT

BAKING
POWDER

Instructions

1. I recommend using metric measurements. In a bowl, mash the banana with a fork, add the other ingredients, and whisk until just combined.

2. Heat a little oil in a skillet over medium heat. Spoon some of the batter (I use one heaping ice cream scoop) into the hot skillet. Cook the pancake over medium-low heat, flipping halfway, until golden brown on both sides (a few minutes per side).

3. Serve with fruit, maple syrup, chocolate sauce, caramel sauce, or your favorite toppings. Enjoy!

Notes

- **Oat flour:** If you don't have oat flour, process oats in a blender or electric spice/coffee grinder until floury.

- You can use **buckwheat flour** instead of oat flour. You might need to adjust the amount of plant-based milk, though.

- **Canned coconut milk:** You can use any other plant-based milk instead with the addition of 1 tablespoon of oil.

- **Banana:** Applesauce might also work in this recipe.

BREAKFAST GRANOLA CUPS

10 minutes, 8 servings

GRANOLA CUPS

1½ cups (170 g/6 oz) granola

½ cup (65 g/2.3 oz) sunflower seeds
or chopped nuts of choice

2 Tbsp (40 g/1.4 oz) agave syrup
(or maple syrup)

3 Tbsp (50 g/1.8 oz) sunflower seed
butter or nut butter of choice

1 pinch of salt

FILLING

¼ cup (60 g/2.1 oz) sunflower seed
butter (melted) or nut butter of choice

TOPPING

½ cup (90 g/3.2 oz) dairy-free
chocolate chips (or dark chocolate,
chopped)

Instructions

1. I recommend using metric measurements. Combine all the granola cup ingredients in a large bowl and mix well. The mixture should stick together when pressed between your fingers. If it's not sticky enough, add a little more sweetener.

2. Grease a muffin/cupcake pan or use a silicone mold. Then, divide the mixture between the pan "cups" using a tablespoon measuring spoon to press the mixture into the cup and create a dent in the middle of each "cup."

3. Put a heaped teaspoon of sunflower seed butter into the center of each granola cup. Freeze until firm, about 60 minutes.

4. Melt the chocolate chips in a double boiler, optionally with 1–2 tsp of coconut oil.

5. Once the chocolate has melted, pour it over the sunflower seed butter on each granola cup. It will harden quickly because the sunflower seed butter is cold.

6. Store them in the fridge for several days or in the freezer for 2–3 months.

GRANOLA

SUNFLOWER
SEEDS

AGAVE
SYRUP

SUNFLOWER
SEED BUTTER

SALT

DAIRY-FREE
CHOCOLATE

SIMPLE BLISS BALLS

5 minutes, 12 balls

1 cup (130 g/4.6 oz) sunflower
    seeds (see notes)
¼ cup (20 g/0.7 oz) oats (gluten-free
    if needed, see notes)
120 g (4.25 oz) pitted dates (see notes)
1 tsp vanilla extract

OPTIONAL INGREDIENTS
Peanut butter (or sunflower seed
    butter), to fill
Desiccated coconut, to roll

SUNFLOWER
SEEDS

OATS

DATES

VANILLA
EXTRACT

Instructions

1. Process the sunflower seeds and oats in a food processor for 10–20 seconds.

2. Add the dates and the vanilla extract, and blend again until the mixture holds together when pressed between your fingers. If it's too dry, add a few more dates.

3. Use about 1 Tbsp (20 g) of the mixture to roll a ball between your hands. Optionally fill with ½ tsp of nut/seed butter of choice. Continue until no dough remains.

4. I rolled the balls in desiccated coconut, but you can roll them in cocoa powder, matcha powder, powdered sugar, cinnamon, or maqui berry powder.

Notes

- **Sunflower Seeds:** You can use any nuts instead.

- **Oats:** Use the ground nuts or seeds of choice instead of oats for a raw vegan version.

- **Dates:** You can use other dried fruit, such as dried figs, dried apricots, etc., instead of dates.

HEALTHY BREAKFAST COOKIES

25 minutes, 18 cookies

1½ cups (150 g/5.3 oz) rolled oats
(gluten-free if needed)

4 Tbsp (24 g/0.8 oz) ground sunflower
seeds (or use almond flour)

½ cup (65 g/2.3 oz) sunflower seeds

¼ cup (36 g/1.3 oz) pumpkin seeds

3 Tbsp (34 g/1.2 oz) chia seeds

4 Tbsp (36 g/1.3 oz) hemp seeds (or
use sesame seeds)

¼ cup (36 g/1.3 oz) peanuts (or
nuts/seeds of choice)

2 pinches of salt

1 tsp cinnamon

¼ cup (34 g/1.2 oz) raisins

¼ cup (34 g/1.2 oz) dried cranberries

⅜ cup (120 g/4.2 oz) maple syrup

⅓ cup (80 g/2.8 oz) tahini

1 Tbsp ground flax seeds +
3 Tbsp water

Instructions

1. Line a baking sheet with parchment paper and preheat the oven to 350°F (177°C). At the same time, prepare the flax egg by combining the ground flaxseed and water, mixing well, and setting it aside for 5 minutes.

2. Add all the dry ingredients to a bowl and stir to combine.

3. Add the wet ingredients (including the flax egg) and mix thoroughly.

4. Spoon the batter onto the baking sheet, using a tablespoon per cookie.

5. Bake for 15–18 minutes, then allow to cool completely and enjoy!

Notes

- **Mix and match nuts and seeds:** These healthy cookies are super versatile, so use whatever nuts and seeds you have.

- Store any leftovers in a container on the counter for 5–6 days or in the freezer for 2–3 months.

OATS
PEANUTS
SALT
GROUND SUNFLOWER SEEDS
CINNAMON
RAISINS
SUNFLOWER SEEDS
DRIED CRANBERRIES
PUMPKIN SEEDS
MAPLE SYRUP
CHIA SEEDS
TAHINI
HEMP SEEDS
GROUND FLAX SEEDS

BREAKFAST BURRITOS

45 minutes, 8 servings

ROASTED POTATOES

4–5 medium-sized (600 g/21.2 oz)
    potatoes
½ Tbsp oil
½ tsp onion powder
¼ tsp smoked paprika
¼ tsp cumin seeds
Salt and black pepper to taste

BURRITOS

1 avocado, sliced
1 can (425 g/15 oz) kidney beans (or
    other beans), drained and rinsed
1 green pepper, chopped (or color
    of choice)
2 tomatoes, chopped
140 g (4.9 oz) fresh mushrooms, sliced
1 onion, chopped
2 garlic cloves, minced
2–3 Tbsp red cabbage, shredded
4 flour tortillas, gluten-free if needed
½ Tbsp oil
1 tsp oregano
¾ tsp ground cumin
½ tsp onion powder
⅓ tsp smoked paprika
Salt and black pepper to taste

CASHEW SAUCE

2 Tbsp (32 g/1.1 oz) cashew butter
Juice of ½ lime
Enough water to thin out
⅓ tsp onion powder
¼ tsp garlic powder
Hot sauce to taste
Salt and black pepper to taste

Instructions

Roasted Potatoes

1. Preheat the oven to 400°F (205°C) and line a baking sheet with parchment paper.

2. Chop the potatoes into 1-inch (2.5 cm) cubes and add them to a bowl with the seasonings and oil.

3. Toss well to coat, and transfer the potatoes to the prepared baking sheet. Bake them in the oven for 30 minutes, or until cooked through and golden brown.

Cashew Sauce

1. To make the cashew sauce, simply whisk the ingredients in a small bowl until smooth and creamy.

Burritos

1. While the potatoes are in the oven, chop the mushrooms, onion, garlic, tomatoes, pepper, avocado, and red cabbage.

2. Heat ½ Tbsp oil in a skillet, and add onion, mushrooms, and pepper. Cook over medium heat for 5 minutes. Then, add the spices, garlic, and tomatoes and cook for a further 1–2 minutes.

3. Toast the tortillas one at a time (in a pan) and place 2–3 Tbsp of the veggie mixture, the beans, the roasted potatoes, the avocado, a little red cabbage, and cashew sauce per tortilla.

4. Roll the burritos up by folding the sides inward and the edge closest to you over the filling, pulling tightly.

5. Finally, toast the burritos in a pan for a few minutes per side until crunchy and golden brown, and enjoy!

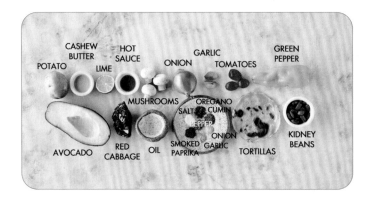

STRAWBERRY CRUMB BARS

45 minutes, 10 servings

DOUGH

2 cups (180 g/6.3 oz) rolled oats,
   gluten-free if needed

1 cup (120 g/4.2 oz) almond flour
   (see notes)

1 cup (90 g/3.2 oz) oat flour,
   gluten-free if needed

1 small (80 g/2.8 oz) banana
   (weight without peel), mashed (see
   notes)

¼ cup (80 g/2.8 oz) maple syrup or
   agave syrup

¼ cup (60 ml/2.1 oz) canned
   coconut milk (see notes)

2 tsp baking powder

STRAWBERRY FILLING

3 cups (450 g/15.9 oz) diced
   strawberries

⅓ cup (105 g/3.7 oz) maple syrup
   or agave syrup

2–3 tsp lime or lemon juice

5 tsp chia seeds

3 tsp potato starch or cornstarch

Instructions

1. I recommend using metric measurements. Preheat the oven to 360°F (180°C).

2. Transfer the ingredients for the strawberry filling to a saucepan, bring to a boil, and let it simmer over low heat for 5–10 minutes, stirring occasionally.

3. Meanwhile, mix all ingredients for the dough in a bowl with a hand mixer.

4. Press ⅔ of the dough evenly into a greased or lined baking dish, around 7x11 inches (18x28 cm).

5. Pour the strawberry filling over the crust.

6. Crumble the remaining ⅓ of the dough on top.

7. Bake in the oven for 20–25 minutes. Enjoy!

Notes

- **Banana:** Use banana or applesauce for a low-fat version. If you prefer a flaky/buttery soft crust, use 40 grams of banana (or applesauce) with **40 grams of vegan butter (or margarine)**.

- **Almond flour:** You can use any ground nuts/seeds of choice (e.g., hazelnuts, shredded unsweetened coconut) instead of almond flour.

- **Coconut milk:** You could use oat cream or soy cream instead.

- Store leftovers covered in the fridge for up to 5 days.

CHOCOLATE MUFFINS

40 minutes, 9–10 muffins

DRY INGREDIENTS

1⅓ cup (120 g/4.2 oz) oat flour, gluten-free if needed (see notes)

⅓–½ cup (70–100 g/2.5–3.5 oz) coconut sugar (see notes)

½ cup (50 g/1.8 oz) unsweetened cocoa powder (see notes)

1 tsp baking powder

¼ tsp baking soda

¼ tsp salt

½ cup (90 g/3.2 oz) chocolate chips (dairy-free) + more for the top

WET INGREDIENTS

¾ cup (180 ml/6.3 oz) plant-based milk of choice

⅔ cup (160 g/5.6 oz) applesauce, unsweetened (see notes)

¼ cup (65 g/2.3 oz) nut butter (see notes)

1 Tbsp apple cider vinegar or lemon juice

1 tsp vanilla extract

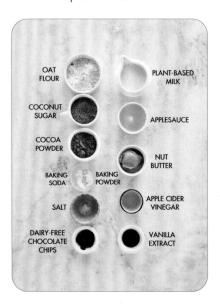

Instructions

1. I recommend using metric measurements. Line a muffin pan with paper liners (or grease the pan) and preheat the oven to 360°F (180°C).

2. Add all the dry ingredients (except the chocolate chips) to a large mixing bowl and whisk.

3. Then, add the wet ingredients and stir with a fork to combine. You can also use a hand mixer.

4. Finally, stir in the vegan chocolate chips.

5. Divide the batter among the wells of the muffin pan. I had enough batter to make 10 muffins.

6. Bake for 25–30 minutes or until you spot cracks on top of the muffins and a toothpick inserted into the center of the muffin comes out almost clean (it's okay if the toothpick is crumbly/slightly sticky, but it shouldn't come out wet).

7. Let the muffins cool and enjoy!

Notes

- **Oat flour:** You can use millet flour instead.

- **Sweetener:** Any granulated sweetener can be used (e.g., organic white sugar, date sugar, or even Erythritol). I used ⅓ cup in this recipe, however, if you have a sweet tooth, I recommend using ½ cup.

- **Cocoa powder:** You can use carob powder instead.

- **Applesauce:** You can use mashed banana instead.

- **Nut butter:** You can use almond butter, cashew butter, peanut butter, etc. Use sunflower seed butter for a nut-free version. If you don't have nut butter, use 4 Tbsp oil instead.

- Store any leftovers in an airtight container in the fridge for 5 days or in the freezer for up to 3 months.

HEALTHY BANANA BREAD

55 minutes, 10 slices

DRY INGREDIENTS

⅔ cup (100 g/3.5 oz) gluten-free
    flour (see notes)

1 cup (90 g/3.2 oz) oat flour
    (gluten-free if needed)

⅝ cup (70 g/2.5 oz) ground seeds
    or nuts of choice

1 ½ tsp baking powder

¼ tsp salt

WET INGREDIENTS

3 small (240 g/8.5 oz) ripe bananas
    (weight without peel) + 1 for the top

1 tsp vanilla extract

½ Tbsp lemon juice or vinegar

½ cup (100 g/3.5 oz) pitted dates,
    chopped

⅔ cup (160 ml/5.6 oz)
    plant-based milk

Optional: 3 Tbsp chopped dairy-
    free chocolate (I use sugar-free)

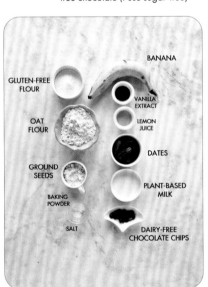

Instructions

1. Preheat the oven to 360°F (180°C) and line an 8-inch baking pan with parchment paper.

2. Add all dry ingredients (except the chocolate) to a large bowl and mix with a spoon.

3. In a different bowl, mash the bananas well with a fork (or use a small blender).

4. Add the vanilla extract, vinegar, dates, and plant-based milk and stir well.

5. Transfer the wet ingredients to the dry ones and stir to combine.

6. Pour the batter into the baking pan and optionally add the chocolate on top.

7. Bake the banana bread in the oven for about 45 minutes. Check the center with a toothpick—if it comes out dry or slightly sticky/crumbly, that's fine, just not wet.

8. Let the banana bread cool, slice it, and enjoy.

Notes

- **Flour:** I use a gluten-free flour blend consisting of 50 percent buckwheat flour and 50 percent rice flour. However, you can also use an all-purpose GF flour blend or regular flour.

- Store any leftovers in an airtight container in the fridge for 5–6 days or in the freezer for up to 3 months.

VEGGIE OMELETTETE

20 minutes, 2 servings

2 tsp oil

½ medium (50 g/1.8 oz)
  onion, chopped

½ (40 g/1.4 oz) bell pepper,
  chopped

40 g (1.4 oz) fresh mushrooms,
  chopped

⅓ cup (60 g/2.1 oz) red lentils
  ground into flour (see instructions)

2½ Tbsp (20 g/0.7 oz) tapioca
  flour/starch (see notes)

½ tsp salt

½ tsp garlic powder

¼ tsp black pepper

¼ tsp cumin

¼ tsp smoked paprika

1 pinch of kala namak and turmeric

⅔ cup (150 ml/5.3 oz) water

2–3 Tbsp fresh herbs like parsley

Instructions

1. Heat about 2 teaspoons of oil in a large skillet and add the onion, bell pepper, and mushrooms. Sauté for a few minutes until the veggies are softened, then turn off the heat.

2. Meanwhile, grind 60 grams of red lentils (or split mung beans) in an electric coffee/spice grinder (or high-speed blender) until it's flour. You can also use store-bought lentil flour or mung bean flour. Chickpea flour works too.

3. Combine all the dry ingredients (ground lentils, tapioca flour, salt, garlic powder, black pepper, cumin, smoked paprika, kala namak, and turmeric) in a medium-large bowl and stir until combined.

4. Add the water and whisk to combine. Then, add the cooked veggies and fresh herbs (I used parsley in this dish), and stir again. *Allow the batter to sit for 5–10 minutes for a better consistency.*

5. Heat a few teaspoons of oil in the skillet again (use the same one that you used to sauté the veggies, just wipe it clean with a tissue) and pour in half of the batter once the oil is hot.

6. Spread it evenly with a spoon and let the omelette cook over medium heat for about 3–5 minutes, then flip it over with a spatula and repeat on the other side.

7. Repeat this process with the other omelette, serve, and enjoy!

Notes

- You can replace the **tapioca flour** with more ground lentils or split mung beans, but I prefer the texture of the omelette with tapioca flour.

- Feel free to use **other veggies** (e.g., tomatoes, zucchini, broccoli, etc.). Just make sure they aren't too wet. I often also add 2 cloves of minced garlic for more flavor.

CHOCOLATE OATMEAL

10 minutes, 1 serving

OATMEAL

1 small (80–90 g/3 oz) banana
    (weight without peel)

⅔ cup (60 g/2.1 oz) rolled oats
    (gluten-free if needed)

1 ¼ cup (300 ml/10.6 oz)
    dairy-free milk

1 Tbsp peanut butter (or nut/seed
    butter of choice)

3 tsp cocoa powder (or cacao
    powder)

1 pinch of salt

Cinnamon to taste

OPTIONAL TOPPINGS

1 small banana

Dairy-free chocolate chips to top

Nut/seed butter to drizzle

Maple syrup to drizzle

Instructions

1. Mash one banana with a fork and add it to a saucepan with all the other ingredients (except the toppings).

2. Bring the mixture to a boil, reduce the heat, and let it simmer for 4 minutes, stirring occasionally to prevent sticking/scorching.

3. Serve and optionally top with a second banana, a few chocolate chips, and a drizzle of peanut butter (or your favorite toppings). Enjoy!

BANANA

OATS

DAIRY-FREE MILK

PEANUT BUTTER

COCOA POWDER

SALT

CINNAMON

RASPBERRY MUFFINS

40 minutes, 9–10 muffins

DRY INGREDIENTS

1 cup (90 g/3.2 oz) oat flour, gluten-free if needed (see notes)

1 cup (140 g/4.9 oz) gluten-free flour blend or regular flour (see notes)

1 ½ tsp baking powder

¼ tsp baking soda

¼ tsp salt

WET INGREDIENTS

¾ cup (180 ml/6.3 oz) plant-based milk (see notes)

⅓ cup (105 g/3.7 oz) maple syrup or liquid sweetener of choice

2½ Tbsp (30 g/1.1 oz) oil (see notes)

1 Tbsp lemon juice or lime juice

1 ½ tsp vanilla extract

1 ½ cups (150 g/5.3 oz) raspberries, fresh or frozen

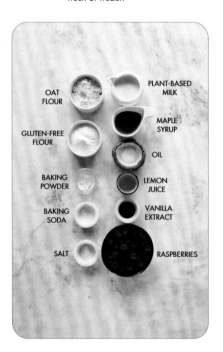

Instructions

1. I recommend using metric measurements. First, preheat the oven to 360°F (180°C) and line a muffin pan with paper liners or grease the pan.

2. Add plant-based milk and lemon juice to a small/medium bowl. Stir to combine and set aside for a few minutes to make "vegan buttermilk."

3. Meanwhile, add all the dry ingredients to a large mixing bowl and whisk.

4. Add the wet ingredients and stir with a spatula or whisk to combine. Do not overmix the batter. Use more milk if the batter thickens too much. Finally, fold in the raspberries.

5. Divide the batter among the wells of the muffin pan. I had enough batter to make 10 muffins.

6. Bake for 25–30 minutes or until you spot cracks on top of the muffins, and a toothpick inserted into the center comes out almost clean (a few crumbs are fine, but not wet).

7. Let the muffins cool and enjoy!

Notes

- **Oat flour:** You can use millet flour instead.

- **Gluten-free flour blend:** I use Bob's Red Mill GF All-purpose 1:1 flour. Any GF flour blend should work fine. Please do **not** use coconut flour, though. If you aren't gluten-free, you can use regular all-purpose flour or spelt flour.

- **Oil:** I use coconut oil, but canola oil should work fine too. If you don't want to use oil, add 3–4 tablespoons of cashew butter instead.

- **Milk:** Any dairy-free milk is fine.

- Store any leftovers in an airtight container in the fridge for 5 days or in the freezer for 3 months.

BLUEBERRY CHIA OATS

10 minutes, 2 servings

BLUEBERRY CHIA OATS

1 cup (90 g/3.2 oz) quick oats
  (gluten-free if needed)

3 Tbsp chia seeds, divided

1 cup (240 ml/8.5 oz) dairy-free
  milk (see notes)

1 cup (150 g/5.3 oz) frozen
  blueberries

2–3 Tbsp sweetener of choice,
  divided (see notes)

TOPPINGS

Fresh blueberries

Granola, shredded coconut, etc.

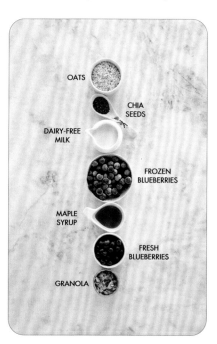

OATS

CHIA
SEEDS

DAIRY-FREE
MILK

FROZEN
BLUEBERRIES

MAPLE
SYRUP

FRESH
BLUEBERRIES

GRANOLA

Instructions

1. Add the oats, 2 Tbsp of chia seeds, dairy-free milk, and 1–2 Tbsp of sweetener to a medium bowl and stir to combine. Set aside.

2. Add the frozen blueberries, 1 Tbsp of chia seeds, and 1 Tbsp of sweetener to a saucepan or skillet and bring the mixture to a simmer. Using a spatula, gently press the blueberries to release their juices.

3. Then, reduce the heat to low and let the blueberries simmer for about 5 minutes, or until the mixture thickens.

4. Finally, divide the oat and blueberry mixtures between two glasses, layering oats first, then blueberries, and then another layer of oats.

5. Enjoy it immediately, or chill the jars in the fridge for 20 minutes (or longer, e.g., overnight).

Notes

- **Dairy-free milk:** Any milk is fine such as almond, coconut, oat, etc.

- **Sweetener:** I use maple syrup, but you can use any sweetener of your choice, granulated or liquid.

SIDES & SALADS

SCALLOPED POTATOES

20 minutes, 6–8 servings

CASHEW SAUCE

1⅔ cups (400 ml / 14.1 oz) plant-
    based milk of choice

1⅔ cups (400 ml / 14.1 oz) vegetable
    broth

1 cup (150 g / 5.3 oz) cashews,
    soaked

2 Tbsp (15 g / 0.5 oz) tapioca flour/
    starch or arrowroot flour

½ cup (30 g / 1.1 oz) nutritional yeast

½ tsp paprika

Ground black pepper to taste

1¼ tsp salt (or less/more to taste)

1 tsp onion powder

3–4 garlic cloves

OTHER INGREDIENTS

1400 g (49.4 oz) Yukon Gold
    potatoes (about 7–8 medium)

1 medium onion

Fresh herbs to garnish

Instructions

1. First, soak the cashews in boiling water for about 15 minutes, then drain.

2. Meanwhile, peel the potatoes and slice them thinly (about ⅛-inch thick) with a knife or mandoline. You will need (1400 g) of peeled potatoes. Also, peel and thinly slice the onion.

3. Preheat the oven to 400°F (205°C) and grease a 9x13-inch (23x33 cm) baking dish. Set aside.

4. To make the cashew sauce, add all the sauce ingredients to a blender. Blend on high until completely smooth (1–2 minutes). The sauce will be very thin at first but thickens as it bakes. Taste the sauce and add more salt/pepper/spices if needed.

5. Transfer half of the potatoes to the prepared baking dish and pour half the sauce over them.

6. Spread the sliced onion on top, and layer the remaining potatoes over the onion. Pour the remaining sauce into the baking dish.

7. Bake for about 60–70 minutes. The baking time depends on the thickness of the sliced potatoes. The potatoes should be fork-tender and golden brown when ready.

8. Allow it to cool for 5–10 minutes, then garnish with fresh parsley or chives. Enjoy!

BUFFALO CAULIFLOWER WINGS

25 minutes, 4 servings

BATTER

½ heaped cup (60 g/2.1 oz)
   chickpea flour (see notes)

¼ cup (60 ml/2.1 oz) dairy-free milk

¼ cup (60 g/2.1 oz) spicy hot sauce

1 tsp onion powder

1 tsp garlic powder

½ tsp salt

½ tsp smoked paprika

1 Tbsp oil or melted vegan butter

OTHER INGREDIENTS

1 small-medium head (600 g/21.2 oz)
   cauliflower (weight without stem)

Mild hot sauce or ketchup, to brush

Instructions

1. Cut the cauliflower into even-sized florets and transfer them to a large bowl.

2. Add chickpea flour to a medium bowl along with the dairy-free milk, hot sauce, spices, and oil. Whisk to combine.

3. Pour the batter over the cauliflower florets and toss thoroughly to combine, using tongs, a spoon, or even your fingers. *If you prefer crispy cauliflower wings, coat the florets with some breadcrumbs (regular or gluten-free) too.*

4. Spray the bottom of your air fryer with oil and add the coated cauliflower florets. Spread them evenly in a single layer with space between (to ensure they become crispy).

5. Cook at 370°F (188°C) for 15 minutes. Transfer the cauliflower florets to a plate and brush each one with either more hot sauce (if you like it spicy) or use ketchup.

Notes

- **Flour:** I love chickpea flour, but regular all-purpose flour will also work. Replace 1 Tbsp of the flour with cornstarch for crispier batter.

- **Batter:** The batter is enough for a small/medium head of cauliflower, weighing 600 grams without the stem. If you use a large cauliflower (about 900 g), double the batter ingredients.

- **Baked method:** You could also bake the cauliflower wings in the oven at 425°F (220°C), but the cooking time will increase to about 40 minutes (flipping halfway through).

SMASHED POTATOES

45 minutes, 3–4 servings

900 g (31.7 oz) small potatoes

½ Tbsp salt for boiling + more for
sprinkling

1½ Tbsp oil for brushing

Onion powder, garlic powder, and
black pepper to sprinkle (optional)

Fresh parsley to garnish

POTATOES

OIL

GARLIC
POWDER

SALT

ONION
POWDER

PEPPER

PARSLEY

Instructions

1. Heat water in a large pot, stir in the salt, and add the potatoes (they should be covered with at least 1 inch/2.5 cm of water). Cook the potatoes for about 20 minutes or until fork-tender, then drain the water. The time depends on the size of the potatoes.

2. If you plan on making the smashed potatoes in your oven, then also preheat your oven to 400°F (205°C) now.

3. Transfer the cooked potatoes to a large greased baking sheet and smash each potato using the flat bottom of a glass.

4. Brush the smashed potatoes with the oil, sprinkle them with salt, and bake for 35–45 minutes or until golden (they might be done earlier, depending on your oven). Broil at the end for 1–2 minutes for extra crispiness. Alternatively, cook them in an air fryer for 15–18 minutes at 380°F (190°C).

5. Sprinkle with black pepper, onion powder, and garlic powder (optional). Garnish with fresh parsley and enjoy with avocado pesto (page 39).

Notes

- **Salt the water liberally:** Potatoes require a lot of salt to absorb a good amount of flavor, so don't be shy.

- **Don't skimp on oil:** This will cling to all the fluffy smashed edges and help your roasted smashed potatoes become super crispy.

POTATO FLATBREAD

40 minutes, 8 servings

3 medium-large (400 g/14.1 oz) Yukon Gold potatoes (see instructions)

¾ cup + 1 Tbsp (80 g/2.8 oz) chickpea flour (see notes)

5 Tbsp (40 g/1.4 oz) tapioca flour/starch

1 tsp baking powder

½–¾ tsp salt

1 pinch of nutmeg

1 Tbsp oil + more to fry

⅓ cup scallions, chopped

POTATOES

CHICKPEA FLOUR

TAPIOCA FLOUR

BAKING POWDER

SALT   NUTMEG

OIL

SCALLIONS

Instructions

1. Boil the potatoes in salted water until they are fork-tender, then drain the water, let the potatoes cool, and peel them. You need 400 grams (14.1 oz) of potato after cooking and peeling. Mash them in a bowl with a potato masher or a potato ricer.

2. Add the flours, baking powder, salt, nutmeg, oil, and scallions. Mix it with a spoon first, then use your hands to knead the dough. You will have to add more flour a spoonful at a time until the dough isn't sticky.

3. Divide the dough into 6–8 parts and roll them into balls. Make 8 for smaller, thinner flatbreads and 6 for slightly larger/thicker ones.

4. With a rolling pin, roll out each ball between 2 sheets of oiled wax paper (or parchment paper) into a disc, between ⅛-inch and ¼-inch thick and 5 ½–6 inches in diameter.

5. Lightly oil a large nonstick frying pan/skillet over medium heat. Once ready, remove the top layer of wax paper from the first potato flatbread and flip it over onto the pan, peeling away the remaining layer of wax paper.

6. Cook the flatbread over medium heat for about 3–4 minutes, flip it over, and cook for a further 2 minutes. Place the cooked flatbread on a plate and cover it with a kitchen towel. While one flatbread cooks, you can roll out the next dough ball and repeat the process.

7. Brush them with a little garlic oil/butter, sprinkle with more fresh herbs, and enjoy!

Notes

- **Flour:** If you aren't gluten-free, you can use 1 cup of regular all-purpose flour instead of chickpea and tapioca flour; however, you might need to add more flour if the dough is too sticky.

- It's important to cook the potatoes with the peel so they don't absorb too much water. You can also cook them a day ahead or use leftover mashed potatoes for a quick flatbread!

GLUTEN-FREE GNOCCHI

45 minutes, 6 servings

1000 g (35.3 oz) potatoes (e.g.,
    Yukon Gold), peeled and chopped
1¾–2 ¼ cups (180–240 g/6.3–8.5
    oz) chickpea flour
1 cup (120 g/4.2 oz) tapioca flour/
    starch + more for dusting (see notes)
½ tsp salt

POTATOES

CHICKPEA
FLOUR

TAPIOCA
FLOUR

SALT

Instructions

1. I recommend using metric measurements. Peel and chop the potatoes, transfer them to a pot with salted water, and bring to a boil. Cook over medium heat for about 15 minutes or until tender, then drain thoroughly. Transfer the potatoes back to the pot and mash with a potato masher or ricer (don't use a food processor or blender or they'll become gummy).

2. Add 1 ¾ cups of chickpea flour and tapioca flour, and knead with your hands until a dough forms.

3. The dough may still be a bit sticky, but it should be fine to handle. If the dough is too sticky, add more chickpea flour and knead again. It depends on the type of potato whether you will need 1 ¾ cups or over 2 cups of chickpea flour.

4. Cut the dough into equally sized pieces and dust with tapioca flour.

5. With your fingers, roll each piece into ropes. Next, use a knife to cut the dough into 1-inch pieces and form them into small balls with your hands. You can roll every ball over the back of a fork if you want ridges on your gnocchi (this step is optional but is great for picking up sauce).

6. Add the gnocchi to a pot of salted boiling water. Once the gnocchi rise to the surface (usually only 2–4 minutes), remove them with a slotted spoon.

7. Serve the homemade gnocchi with your sauce of choice, or sauté them for a few minutes in a pan with a little bit of vegan butter or oil until crispy. Enjoy!

Notes

• You can use arrowroot flour, potato starch, or cornstarch instead of tapioca flour. I had the best result with tapioca flour, though.

• **Make ahead:** Lay the uncooked gnocchi on a tray (with space between) and freeze until solid. Transfer to a large freezer bag/container for 2 months, or store them covered in the fridge for 1–2 days. You can then cook the gnocchi from frozen, but do so in smaller batches. Or let them thaw for a few minutes (not too long, or they'll go mushy) first.

LYONNAISE POTATOES

35 minutes, 2 servings

1 medium onion

2 Tbsp oil, divided

450 g (15.9 oz) potatoes
   (e.g. Yukon Gold)

½ tsp garlic powder

½ tsp paprika

½ tsp ground cumin

½ tsp salt

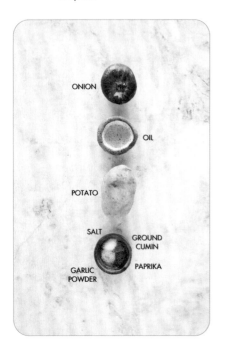

Instructions

1. Slice the onion into thin rounds and sauté in 1 Tbsp heated oil in a skillet. Cook them over medium heat until caramelized (about 15 minutes), adding a few spoons of water after about 5 and 10 minutes to help with the caramelization process, stirring in between. Then, remove the caramelized onions from the skillet.

2. Meanwhile, slice the potatoes (¼-inch resp. 0.6–0.7 cm thick). Add the potato slices to a pot, cover with salted water, and bring it to a boil over high heat. Once boiling, reduce the heat to low-medium and let the potatoes simmer for 4–5 minutes. Then, drain the water and dry the potatoes with a kitchen towel.

3. Heat 1 Tbsp oil in the same skillet you used for the onions and add the cooked potatoes. Cook for about 10–15 minutes over medium heat, or until the potatoes are crisp and golden brown.

4. Add the caramelized onions and the spices and cook for a further few minutes.

5. Serve and garnish with fresh parsley. Enjoy!

STUFFED ZUCCHINI

50 minutes, 4 servings

2 medium zucchini

½ Tbsp vegetable oil or water

1 small/medium onion, chopped

2–3 garlic cloves, minced

1 small bell pepper, chopped

1 tsp onion powder

1 tsp coconut sugar or sweetener of
choice

½ tsp smoked paprika

½ tsp ground cumin

Salt, ground black pepper, and chili
powder to taste

1 Tbsp GF soy sauce, tamari, or
coconut aminos

1 Tbsp rice vinegar

1 heaped Tbsp tomato paste

1 Tbsp hot sauce (or more to taste)

4–6 Tbsp plant-based milk

1 can (425 g/15 oz) chickpeas,
drained and rinsed

1 batch of vegan cheese sauce (page
31) or 7.1 oz (200 g) store-bought
vegan cheese

Fresh herbs to garnish

Instructions

1. Cut the zucchini in half (lengthwise) and scoop out ⅔ of the flesh, leaving a ½-inch (1 cm) thick border around the skin. Chop the scooped-out zucchini with a knife and set it aside.

2. Meanwhile, heat oil in a skillet over medium heat. Add onion and sauté for about 4 minutes.

3. Add garlic, bell pepper, zucchini flesh, the spices, soy sauce, rice vinegar, tomato paste, hot sauce, and plant-based milk. Put a lid on the skillet and cook for about 10 minutes, stirring occasionally.

4. Meanwhile, prepare the vegan cheese sauce or use store-bought vegan cheese.

5. At the same time, preheat the oven to 410°F (210°C) and line a large baking sheet with parchment paper.

6. Add the chickpeas to the skillet and cook for a few more minutes. Taste and adjust any of the seasonings. Then, stuff each zucchini halfway with the chickpea mixture.

7. Add the vegan cheese on top and bake for 20–25 minutes in the oven. Garnish with fresh herbs and enjoy!

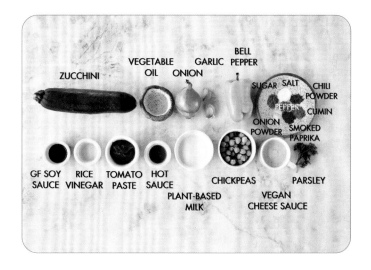

POTATO DUMPLINGS

50 minutes, 6–8 servings

800 g (28.2 oz) potatoes (see notes)

120 g (4.2 oz) potato starch
(see notes)

¾–1 tsp salt

1 pinch of nutmeg

**MUSHROOM STUFFING
(OPTIONAL)**

200 g (7.1 oz) fresh mushrooms,
chopped

½ medium onion, diced

2 garlic cloves, minced

½ Tbsp GF soy sauce, tamari, or
coconut aminos

Onion powder, smoked paprika, cumin,
salt, and black pepper to taste

Instructions

1. Cook the potatoes (peel on) in a large pot of boiling salted water until fork-tender, then drain the water.

2. Allow them to cool, then peel the potatoes (the weight of the cooked and peeled potatoes should be 750 g or 26.5 oz). Mash them with a potato masher.

3. Add potato starch, salt, and nutmeg. Use your hands to knead the mixture into a smooth dough. Meanwhile, bring salted water to a simmer in a large pot.

4. Wet your hands, take a handful of dough, and shape it into a ball. The recipe makes 6–8 potato dumplings, depending on how large you make them. You can fill some of them or leave them all plain. (see below for my mushroom stuffing recipe

5. Reduce the heat of the pot. The water should be hot (about 80–85°C/176–185°F), but **it shouldn't boil or simmer.** Carefully add the potato balls into the pot and let them cook in the water for 15 minutes until they rise to the surface.

6. Remove them from the water with a slotted spoon. Serve and enjoy!

Instructions for Mushroom Stuffing (optional)

1. Pan-fry the mushrooms and onion in a skillet until softened, about 5 minutes. Add all remaining ingredients and sauté for a further minute.

Notes

- **Potatoes:** It's best to use all-purpose potatoes like **Yukon Gold** or starchy potatoes like Russet. If you use waxy potatoes, you'll need to use more potato starch. If the mixture turns out too dry, add a little water.

- **Potato starch** is my go-to for this recipe, though you could also use tapioca flour/starch or cornstarch.

- The potato dumplings are a bit sticky/gooey initially (especially the ones made with tapioca flour/starch), but they firm up nicely once they cool.

- It's imperative that the **water doesn't boil.** Otherwise, the dumplings might fall apart and become mushy!

- Serve with vegan meatloaf (page 157) and mushroom gravy (page 35).

MASHED POTATOES

30 minutes, 4 servings

1000 g (35.3 oz) potatoes (Yukon
    Gold or Russet)

½ cup (120 ml/4.2 oz) dairy-free
    milk (see notes)

Up to ½ cup (120 ml/4.2 oz)
    reserved cooking water

1 ½–2 tsp salt, divided

Black pepper and ground nutmeg to
    taste (see notes)

Fresh herbs to garnish (e.g., chives)

1–2 Tbsp olive oil (or more to taste)
    (see notes)

Instructions

1. Peel and slice the potatoes into 2-inch (5 cm) pieces and add them to a large pot. Pour in water to cover the potatoes by a few inches, and add about 1 tsp of salt. Bring to a boil and cook the potatoes covered for around 15 minutes, or until fork-tender.

2. Drain the water from the pot, but reserve about ½ cup of the cooking water. Mash the potatoes with a potato masher (or a potato ricer).

3. Pour in the plant-based milk a little at a time, mashing in between. Also, add salt, pepper, and nutmeg. Then, add the reserved cooking water gradually, while mashing, until you reach a creamy consistency.

4. Taste it and add more salt/pepper or nutmeg if needed, and optionally a little olive oil or dairy-free butter for richness.

5. Garnish with fresh chives, drizzle with olive oil, and serve. Enjoy with lentil stew (page 121).

Notes

- **Milk:** I always use canned lite coconut milk. You can use any other plant-based milk of choice, but the mash won't be as creamy.

- **Nutmeg:** Trust me! I am German, and Germans *always* season potatoes with nutmeg. Use just a pinch at first. You can always add more.

- **Oil:** For this recipe, I used extra virgin olive oil to drizzle. You can also add it directly to the mash, especially if you use low-fat milk. Alternatively, use vegan butter instead of oil.

- **Optional add-ins:** Try roasted garlic for additional flavor!

LEMON VINAIGRETTE

5 minutes, 4 servings

2 Tbsp lemon juice (see notes)

2 tsp Dijon mustard

1 garlic clove, minced or pressed

½ tsp coconut sugar or
   sweetener choice

⅜ tsp salt (or less/more to taste)

Black pepper to taste

1 Tbsp chopped chives

3½ Tbsp (45 g/1.6 oz)
   extra virgin olive oil

1½ Tbsp water (optional,
   if using a blender)

LEMON
MUSTARD
GARLIC
COCONUT
SUGAR
PEPPER
SALT
CHIVES
OLIVE OIL

Instructions

1. Add the lemon juice, mustard, garlic, coconut sugar, salt, pepper, and chopped chives to a jar or mug and whisk well.

2. Slowly add in the olive oil and keep whisking until the dressing is emulsified.

3. For a creamier dressing, blend the mixture with an immersion blender until creamy and add up to 1 – ½ Tbsp of water.

4. Taste the vinaigrette and adjust any element to your taste, salt, lemon, sugar, etc. Then, pour it over your favorite salad (e.g., quinoa salad found on page 111) and enjoy!

Notes

- You can use white wine vinegar instead of lemon for a more traditional vinaigrette.

QUINOA SALAD

25 minutes, 2 servings

½ cup (90 g/3.2 oz) dry quinoa, rinsed

1 cup (240 ml/8.5 oz) water

½ Tbsp veggie bouillon powder or a mini cube

1 (140 g/4.9 oz) cucumber, chopped

1 small (90 g/3.2 oz) red onion, chopped

1 (100 g/3.5 oz) sweet pepper of your choice (I used green), chopped

2 (150 g/5.3 oz) tomatoes, chopped

1 small (130 g/4.6 oz) zucchini, chopped

¾ cup (130 g/4.6 oz) canned chickpeas, drained and rinsed

Lemon vinaigrette (page 108)

Instructions

1. Add ½ cup rinsed quinoa to a saucepan, cover it with 1 cup of water, and add ½ Tbsp of bouillon powder (or a mini bouillon cube). Bring to a boil, then reduce the heat to low, cover the saucepan with a lid, and let the quinoa simmer until it has absorbed all of the water and is tender (about 15 minutes). Then, let it cool.

2. Meanwhile, chop all the vegetables into small, similar-sized pieces.

3. Add the cooled quinoa, the chopped veggies, and the chickpeas to a medium-large bowl.

4. Drizzle with lemon vinaigrette (or dressing of choice), stir, serve, and enjoy!

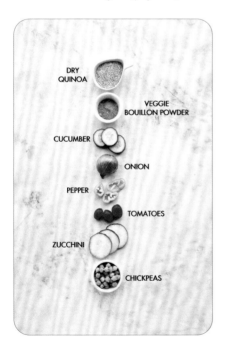

DRY QUINOA

VEGGIE BOUILLON POWDER

CUCUMBER

ONION

PEPPER

TOMATOES

ZUCCHINI

CHICKPEAS

LENTIL SALAD

30 minutes, 4 servings

SALAD

1 cup (200 g/7.1 oz) dried brown
    lentils or green lentils

3 cups (720 ml/25.4 oz) low-sodium
    vegetable broth or water

2 (220 g/7.8 oz) Persian cucumbers

1 (100 g/3.5 oz) sweet pepper
    (color of choice)

½ cup (100 g/3.5 oz) cherry
    tomatoes

1 small (60 g/2.1 oz) red onion

⅓ cup (8 g/0.3 oz) fresh parsley

60 g (2.1 oz) arugula

2 small radishes

¼ (50 g/1.8 oz) apple

⅛ cup (17 g/0.6 oz) sunflower seeds
    or chopped nuts of choice

DRESSING

3 Tbsp (48 g/1.7 oz) creamy tahini

1 Tbsp maple syrup

1 Tbsp Dijon mustard

2 tsp tomato paste

2 Tbsp lime juice

1 Tbsp olive oil

½ tsp garlic powder

Salt and black pepper to taste

2–4 Tbsp water to thin

Instructions

Salad

1. Add the dried lentils, vegetable broth, and (optionally) 1–2 bay leaves to a saucepan. Bring to a boil, then reduce the heat to low and cook for 20 minutes, or until the lentils are soft but not mushy! Drain the lentils using a colander and rinse them with cold water.

2. Meanwhile, dice the cucumbers, sweet pepper, onion, radishes, and apple. Chop the cherry tomatoes in half, and chop the parsley and arugula.

Dressing

1. Add all the dressing ingredients to a bowl or jar and whisk, adding water gradually, depending on how thick/thin you want the dressing to be.

2. Taste it and add more lime juice or seasonings to your liking.

Assembly

1. Add all the salad ingredients to a large plate or bowl, then pour the dressing over it.

2. Toss to combine, then enjoy!

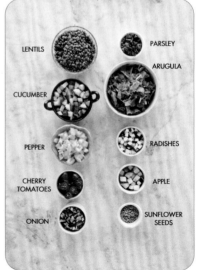

BROWN RICE SALAD

40 minutes, 4 servings

RICE SALAD

1 cup (200 g/7.1 oz) uncooked brown rice

2 cups (480 ml/16.9 oz) vegetable broth or water and salt

1 cup (150 g/5.3 oz) cucumber, diced

1 cup (100 g/3.5 oz) carrots, grated

¾ cup (130 g/4.6 oz) cherry tomatoes, halved

½ (90 g/3.2 oz) bell pepper, diced

½ cup (50 g/1.8 oz) purple cabbage, thinly sliced

1–2 handfuls (40 g/1.4 oz) arugula or lettuce

2 (35 g/1.2 oz) green onions, thinly sliced

¼ cup (30 g/1.1 oz) olives

DRESSING

½ cup (120 g/4.2 oz) vegan sour cream (see notes)

2 Tbsp lemon juice or vinegar of choice

1 Tbsp maple syrup or liquid sweetener of choice

2 tsp olive oil (skip if you prefer it oil-free)

2 tsp Dijon mustard

½ tsp garlic powder

½ tsp dried herbs (optional)

Salt and black pepper to taste

Water to thin

Instructions

Rice

1. Soak the rice in a bowl of lukewarm water for about 15 minutes, then drain. Soaking it longer (e.g., 1 hour) is fine too—it will cook faster then.

2. Bring a pot with 2 cups of vegetable broth (or water and salt) to a boil, add the rice, and cover with a lid. Simmer for about 35 minutes (without stirring), then turn off the heat. Let sit covered for a further 10 minutes, untouched. Then, leave it to cool.

3. Chop the vegetables while the rice cools.

Dressing

- Add all dressing ingredients to a bowl and stir to combine. If you prefer a thinner dressing, add a little water.

Assembly

- Combine all veggies and rice in a salad bowl. Pour the dressing over the salad and serve. Enjoy!

Notes

- **Vegan sour cream:** Alternatively, use vegan mayo or dairy-free yogurt.

MACARONI SALAD

25 minutes, 4 servings

SALAD

250 g (8.8 oz) macaroni (gluten-free
   if needed)

1 red bell pepper, chopped

1 medium-sized onion, diced

3 tomatoes, diced

1 small cucumber, diced

½ cup (70 g/2.5 oz) chopped dill
   pickles

¼ cup (45 g/1.6 oz) olives

OIL-FREE DRESSING

1 can (425 g/15 oz) white beans,
   drained and rinsed

⅔ cup (160 ml/5.6 oz) plant-based
   milk

3 Tbsp cashew butter

2–3 garlic cloves

1 Tbsp Dijon mustard

1 Tbsp lemon juice

1 Tbsp white vinegar

¾ tsp salt and black pepper to taste

Instructions

1. Cook the macaroni according to its package directions.

2. Meanwhile, add the white beans, plant-based milk, cashew butter, garlic, mustard, lime juice, vinegar, salt, and black pepper to a blender. Blend on high speed, scraping down the sides if needed, until the dressing is smooth and creamy. Set aside.

3. In a large bowl, combine the cooled macaroni, chopped pepper, onion, tomatoes, cucumber, dill pickles, and olives. Pour over the dressing and stir to combine.

4. Taste and adjust any of the seasonings (salt/pepper/vinegar).

5. Garnish with fresh herbs (parsley or dill), serve at room temperature or cold, and enjoy! Store leftovers in the fridge for up to 3 days.

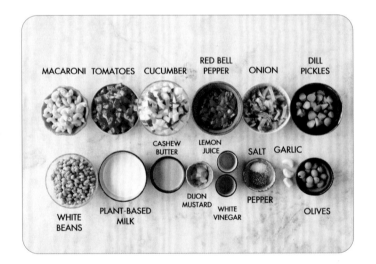

SOUPS, STEWS, & CURRIES

LENTIL STEW

45 minutes, 4 servings

1 cup (200 g/7.1 oz) dried brown
lentils

1 Tbsp oil (for frying)

1 large onion, chopped

2 garlic cloves, minced

135 g (4.8 oz) fresh mushrooms,
sliced

1 tsp each of dried parsley, thyme,
and oregano

3 Tbsp (40 ml/1.4 oz) white wine
(optional)

1 Tbsp balsamic vinegar

2 Tbsp GF soy sauce, tamari, or
coconut aminos

3–4 cups (750–1000 ml/26.5–35.3
oz) vegetable broth

1 large splash full-fat coconut milk (for
extra creaminess)

½ Tbsp cornstarch or arrowroot flour
to thicken (optional)

Salt, black pepper, and chili flakes
to taste

Serve with mashed potatoes
(page 107)

Instructions

1. Rinse the lentils under running water or soak for at least 15 minutes in lukewarm water, then strain and discard the water.

2. Meanwhile, chop the onion, garlic, and mushrooms. Heat oil in a large skillet/frying pan, stir in the onion and garlic and sauté for 3 minutes over medium heat.

3. Add the mushrooms, dried parsley, thyme, oregano, white wine (if used), balsamic vinegar, and soy sauce, and sauté for a further 3–5 minutes.

4. Next, add the lentils and 3–4 cups of vegetable broth and cook over medium-low heat (add more broth for a saucier stew) until the lentils are tender (about 20–25 minutes if soaked beforehand).

5. Once the lentils are tender, mix a generous splash of coconut milk and cornstarch in a small bowl, whisking until lump-free. Add this mixture to the lentil stew and cook for a further minute, or until the desired thickness is reached. Season again with soy sauce (if needed), black pepper, and chili flakes.

6. Serve warm, garnish with chopped pickles and fresh herbs (optional). Enjoy over mashed potatoes (page 107). Store leftovers in an airtight container in the fridge for 3–4 days

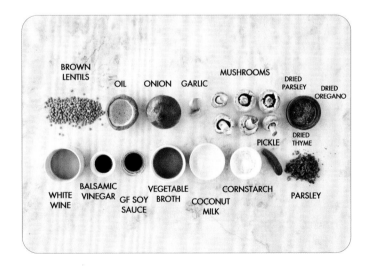

VEGGIE STEW

40 minutes, 4 servings

1 Tbsp oil

1 medium white onion, diced

3 medium (200 g/7.1 oz) carrots, diced

5 small (500 g/17.6 oz) potatoes, chopped

1 medium (70 g/2.5 oz) celery stalk with greens, finely sliced

3 garlic cloves, minced

½–1 Tbsp fresh thyme or 1 tsp dried

½–1 Tbsp fresh rosemary or 1 tsp dried

½–1 Tbsp fresh oregano or 1 tsp dried

1 ½ tsp salt (or to taste)

½ tsp black pepper (or to taste)

⅓ tsp nutmeg

¼ tsp smoked paprika

¼ tsp red pepper flakes or less if sensitive to heat

3 cups (720 ml/25.4 oz) vegetable broth or water

2 ⅓ cup (350 g/12.3 oz) frozen peas

2 Tbsp cornstarch or arrowroot flour

½ cup (120 ml/4.2 oz) dairy-free cream or canned coconut milk

½ cup (120 ml/4.2 oz) white wine or more vegetable broth (see instructions)

Instructions

1. Heat oil over medium heat in a large pan and add the onion. Sauté for 3–4 minutes, stirring frequently.

2. Add the carrots, potatoes, celery, garlic, and all the herbs and spices. Sauté for a further minute, then add the vegetable broth and bring to a boil over high heat.

3. Reduce the heat and cook for about 5 minutes over low-medium heat, then add the frozen peas and cook for 15 more minutes, or until the veggies and peas are softened, stirring occasionally.

4. In a small bowl, mix cornstarch with dairy-free cream or canned coconut milk with a whisk.

5. Pour the cream into the stew and add the white wine (or use more broth/ or plant-based milk for a creamier, alcohol-free soup), and let it simmer for a further 3–4 minutes.

6. Taste and adjust any of the seasonings (salt/pepper/spices) accordingly. You can also optionally blend half of the soup with an immersion blender to make it thicker and creamier.

7. Garnish with fresh herbs (optional) and enjoy!

Notes

- The stew/soup will thicken as it cools. Simply reheat with a generous splash of either vegetable broth or plant-based milk.

- Store leftovers covered in the fridge for up to 3 days.

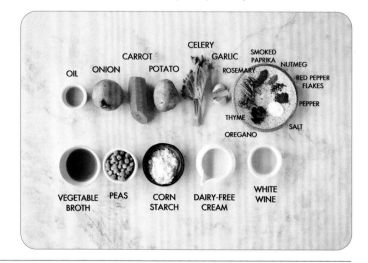

POTATO SOUP

40 minutes, 4 servings

1 Tbsp oil

1 onion, diced

3 garlic cloves, minced

2 celery stalks or ½ small celery root, diced (see notes)

2 small/medium carrots, diced

900 g (31.7 oz) Yukon Gold potatoes, chopped

½ tsp dried marjoram (see notes)

1 pinch of nutmeg

Salt and black pepper to taste

4 cups (1000 ml/35.3 oz) vegetable broth or water

2 whole bay leaves (optional)

⅓ cup (80 ml/2.8 oz) dairy-free cream (see notes)

resh parsley to garnish

OIL · SALT · PEPPER · NUTMEG · DRIED MARJORAM · ONION · GARLIC · CELERY · CARROT · POTATOES · VEGETABLE BROTH · BAY LEAVES · DAIRY-FREE CREAM · PARSLEY

Instructions

1. Heat oil in a large heavy-based pot over medium heat and add the onion. Sauté for 3 minutes, then add the garlic, celery, carrots, potatoes, and all the spices. Sauté for a further minute.

2. Pour in the vegetable broth, add the bay leaves (if used), and bring the soup to a boil.

3. Then, reduce the heat and let the soup simmer for about 20 minutes, covered, or until the vegetables are tender.

4. Transfer half the soup to another pot, remove the bay leaves (if used), and blend one half with an immersion blender until smooth. Alternatively, blend it in a blender, making sure to work in batches, hold down the lid, and avoid overfilling the blender.

5. Pour the blended soup back into the large pot, add the dairy-free cream, and stir to combine. Allow it to simmer for a few more minutes, taste it, and adjust the seasonings (salt/pepper and red pepper flakes for heat) to your liking.

6. Serve in bowls, garnish with fresh parsley, and enjoy!

Notes

- **Celery:** In Germany, it's traditional to use celeriac (celery root). However, if you can't find it, use celery stalks (ribs).

- **Marjoram:** I highly recommend using it as it adds wonderful flavor to this soup. If you don't have it, you can add a little thyme and/or rosemary.

- **Cream:** You can use any dairy-free cream (soy cream, oat cream, cashew cream, or canned coconut milk). Use plant-based milk for a low-fat version.

- Store leftovers covered in the fridge for up to 3 days.

PINTO BEAN SOUP

45 minutes, 6 servings

1 Tbsp olive oil

1 medium onion, diced

1 can (400 g/14 oz) fire-roasted
   tomatoes

3 garlic cloves, minced

2 small (150 g/5.3 oz) carrots,
   peeled and diced

1 medium (135 g/4.8 oz) potato,
   peeled and diced

1 tsp dried oregano

1 tsp ground cumin

1 tsp smoked paprika

Red pepper flakes to taste

2 bay leaves (optional)

2 cups (480 ml/16.9 oz) vegetable
   broth

2 cans (400 g/14 oz each) pinto
   beans, drained and rinsed

Salt and black pepper to taste

Instructions

1. Heat oil in a large, heavy-based pot over medium-high heat. Add the onion and sauté for 4–5 minutes, stirring frequently.

2. Stir in the roasted tomatoes, garlic, carrots, potato, and all the spices. Cook for 1–2 minutes, until fragrant, then pour in the vegetable broth (I also added 2 bay leaves for flavor).

3. Bring the soup to a boil, then reduce the heat to a simmer. Cook it with the lid for 10–15 minutes. Add in the pinto beans and cook for a further 10 minutes or until the veggies are tender, stirring from time to time. Then, turn off the heat.

4. If you notice that too much liquid has evaporated, add more veggie broth or water.

5. Blend about half of the soup (with an immersion blender or in a large blender). Then, pour the blended soup back into the pot and stir to combine.

6. Taste it and adjust the seasonings (salt/pepper/spices) if needed.

7. Serve in bowls and garnish with fresh herbs and optionally a squeeze of lemon or lime juice. Enjoy! Store leftovers covered in the fridge for 3–4 days.

OREGANO

CUMIN

OLIVE OIL

SMOKED
PAPRIKA

RED PEPPER
FLAKES

ONION

BAY LEAVES

ROASTED
TOMATOES

VEGETABLE
BROTH

GARLIC

PINTO
BEANS

CARROT

PEPPER

POTATO

SALT

PUMPKIN SOUP

30 minutes, 4 servings

½ Tbsp oil

1 cup (130 g/4.6 oz) onion, chopped

3 garlic cloves, minced

1½ cups (225 g/7.9 oz) potatoes,
    chopped (peeled)

1½ cups (200 g/7.1 oz) carrots,
    chopped (peeled)

1000 g (35.3 oz) pumpkin, chopped
    (weight without peel and seeds)

1–1½ tsp salt

½ tsp ground ginger

½ tsp ground cumin

¼ tsp ground nutmeg

Black pepper and chili powder to taste

3 cups (720 ml/25.4 oz) vegetable
    broth

½ cup (120 ml/4.2 oz) dairy-free
    cream or full-fat canned coconut milk

Pumpkin seeds for garnish

Instructions

1. Heat oil in a large heavy-based pot and sauté the onion, garlic, potatoes, and carrots over medium heat for about 3 minutes, stirring frequently.

2. Add the pumpkin, all spices, and vegetable broth. Then, stir to combine and bring the mixture to a boil, covered with a lid.

3. Once boiling, reduce the heat to medium and cook for about 12 minutes, until the veggies are tender but not mushy.

4. Remove the pot from the heat and blend the soup with an immersion blender until completely smooth. (Careful, it's hot!) You could also blend it in batches, making sure not to overfill the blender and holding the lid down while blending.

5. Pour in the dairy-free cream and stir, then taste and adjust any of the seasonings accordingly.

6. Serve in bowls, drizzle with more coconut milk, garnish with pumpkin seeds, and enjoy! Store leftovers covered in the fridge for 3–4 days or in the freezer for 3 months.

CREAMY PASTA SOUP

30 minutes, 4 servings

CASHEW CREAM

½ cup (75 g/2.6 oz) cashews soaked
(see notes)

1 can (425 g/15 oz) white beans,
drained and rinsed

1½ cups (360 ml/12.7 oz) plant-
based milk

1 Tbsp lemon juice

¼ tsp salt

SOUP

½ Tbsp oil

1 medium onion, diced

1 large (225 g/7.9 oz) carrot, peeled
and chopped

1–2 (75 g/2.6 oz) celery stalks,
chopped

200 g (7.1 oz) broccoli florets

4 garlic cloves, minced

2 tsp onion powder

2 tsp Italian seasoning

1–2 tsp ground lovage (optional)

Salt and pepper to taste

6 cups (1400 ml/49.4 oz) vegetable
broth

200 g (7.1 oz) pasta of choice (I used
gluten-free)

Fresh herbs to garnish

Instructions

1. Soak the cashews for a couple of hours or boil them for 20 minutes in water until they are soft. Then, transfer them to a blender with the white beans, plant-based milk, lemon juice, and salt. Blend on high speed for about 2 minutes, or until super smooth and creamy. Set aside.

2. Heat oil in a large pot over medium heat and add the onion, carrot, celery, and broccoli. Sauté for about 4 minutes. Then, add the garlic and spices and cook for a further minute.

3. Add the veggie broth, bring to a boil, and then reduce the heat to a simmer.

4. Stir in the cashew cream and allow the soup to simmer for 6–8 minutes.

5. Finally, add the dry pasta of choice and let the soup simmer for a final 8–10 minutes, or until the pasta is al dente (check the package instructions), stirring frequently! *If the soup is too thick, add more veggie broth or plant-based milk!*

6. Taste it and adjust the seasoning to your liking. Finally, garnish with fresh herbs and vegan Parmesan cheese, and enjoy!

Notes

• For a nut-free version, use 75 grams of hemp seeds (no soaking needed)!

THAI COCONUT CURRY SOUP

30 minutes, 5 servings

½ Tbsp oil or water

1 onion, diced

1 Tbsp fresh ginger, minced

4 garlic cloves, minced

1–2 heaped Tbsp Thai red curry paste

1 tsp paprika

½ Tbsp curry powder

¾ tsp ground cumin

¾ tsp turmeric powder

⅓ tsp red pepper flakes

Salt and black pepper to taste

5 cups (1200 ml/42.3 oz) vegetable broth or water

1 ½ cups (360 ml/12.7 oz) canned coconut milk

1–2 Tbsp GF soy sauce, tamari, or coconut aminos

1 Tbsp maple syrup

113 g (4 oz) rice noodles

140 g (4.9 oz) fresh mushrooms, chopped

½ red bell pepper, chopped

Fresh cilantro and sesame seeds to garnish

Fresh lime juice to taste

Instructions

1. Heat oil over medium heat in a large pot or skillet. Add the onion and sauté for 3–4 minutes, then add the ginger and garlic. Sauté for a further minute.

2. Next add the curry paste, spices, vegetable broth (or water), coconut milk, soy sauce, and maple syrup. Stir and bring to a boil over high heat.

3. Add the rice noodles, simmering for 4–6 minutes, or until tender (depending on the thickness of the noodles). Add more veggie broth if the soup gets too thick.

4. Taste and adjust seasonings (salt, pepper, red pepper flakes, sweetener, etc.).

5. Meanwhile, heat a little oil in a pan and sauté the mushrooms and red bell pepper over medium-high heat with a little salt and pepper for about 4–5 minutes.

6. Serve the soup in bowls, and top with the pan-fried mushrooms and bell pepper.

7. Garnish with fresh cilantro and sesame seeds, and drizzle with fresh lemon or lime juice. Enjoy immediately!

Notes

- If you don't want to serve the soup immediately, cook the rice noodles separately and add them before serving. Please note that you should use less vegetable broth when you don't cook the noodles in the soup.

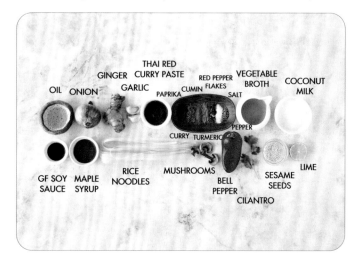

SWEET POTATO CURRY

30 minutes, 4 servings

½ Tbsp oil or water

1 medium (100 g/3.5 oz) onion, chopped

3–4 garlic cloves, minced

2-inch (5 cm) fresh ginger, minced

½ Tbsp curry powder

1 tsp ground turmeric

1 tsp ground cumin

¾ tsp salt (or less/more to taste)

½ tsp smoked paprika

⅛–¼ tsp red pepper flakes

¼ tsp black pepper (or less/more to taste)

¼ tsp ground ginger

1 cup (250 g/8.8 oz) passata (tomato sauce)

450 g (15.9 oz) sweet potatoes, peeled and chopped into 3-cm pieces

1⅓ cup (320 ml/11.3 oz) canned coconut milk

1 can (425 g/15 oz) chickpeas, drained and rinsed (optional)

2 cups (60 g/2.1 oz) fresh spinach

Fresh herbs to garnish (e.g., parsley, cilantro)

Instructions

1. If you want to serve this curry with rice, cook the rice first as per the instructions on the package.

2. Meanwhile, heat oil in a large pot over medium heat and add the onion. Sauté for about 3 minutes.

3. Stir in the garlic and ginger and sauté for a further minute. Add the spices and stir again.

4. Next, add the passata, sweet potato chunks, and coconut milk. Mix and bring to a boil.

5. Reduce the heat to low and simmer for 10–15 minutes, or until the sweet potato chunks are fork-tender and the curry has thickened. **Optional:** Add cooked chickpeas now for additional protein.

6. Finally, add the spinach and let it simmer (lid on) until wilted. Taste and adjust seasonings (salt, pepper, red pepper flakes, etc.) to your liking.

7. Serve with rice or naan bread. Enjoy! Store leftovers covered in the fridge for 3–4 days or in the freezer for 3 months.

RED LENTIL DAHL

30 minutes, 6 servings

1 ½ cups (300 g/10.6 oz) dried red lentils

½ Tbsp vegetable oil

1 large onion, chopped

1 heaped Tbsp fresh ginger, minced

4 garlic cloves, minced

1 large (200 g/7.1 oz) carrot, finely diced

1 small bell pepper, chopped

1 ½ tsp ground cumin

1 Tbsp curry powder

½ Tbsp coconut sugar or sweetener of choice

1 tsp ground turmeric

1 tsp paprika

Salt and black pepper to taste

⅓ tsp red pepper flakes (optional)

3 cups (720 ml/25.4 oz) vegetable broth or water

1 cup (240 ml/8.5 oz) canned coconut milk

Instructions

1. Rinse the lentils under running water. Then, chop the onion, garlic, ginger, bell pepper, and carrot.

2. Heat oil in a large heavy-based pot and sauté the onion for 3–4 minutes over medium heat. Then, add the ginger, garlic, carrot, and bell pepper, and stir.

3. Add the spices, sweetener, lentils, and 3 cups of vegetable broth or water. Bring to a boil and leave to simmer for about 10 minutes.

4. Add the coconut milk and cook for 5 minutes, or until it's reached your desired thickness.

5. Finally, season with salt and black pepper, and adjust any of the other seasonings accordingly.

6. Serve warm with basmati rice, potatoes, or naan, and garnish with fresh herbs. Store leftovers covered in the fridge for 3–4 days or in the freezer for up to 3 months.

MUSHROOM VEGGIE SOUP

35 minutes, 2–3 servings

1 ½ Tbsp vegetable oil

1 medium onion, diced

2 large garlic cloves, minced

450 g (15.9 oz) fresh mushrooms, sliced

1 large stalk leek

1 medium carrot

2 Tbsp fresh tarragon or 1 Tbsp rosemary, chopped

1 Tbsp fresh thyme, chopped

Salt and black pepper to taste

1 Tbsp nutritional yeast

2 ½ cups (600 ml/21.2 oz) vegetable broth

⅓ cup (80 ml/2.8 oz) white wine (or use more vegetable broth)

1 tsp GF soy sauce, tamari, or coconut aminos

¾ cup (180 ml/6.3 oz) dairy-free cream

3–4 Tbsp cornstarch or arrowroot flour

6 Tbsp water

Fresh parsley, chopped for garnish

Instructions

1. Heat the oil over medium heat in a large heavy-based pot and add the diced onion. Sauté for about 3 minutes, stirring frequently.

2. Add the garlic, mushrooms, leek, and carrot and cook for a few minutes until the mushrooms are browned.

3. Stir in the tarragon (or rosemary), thyme, salt, black pepper, and nutritional yeast. Also, pour in the vegetable broth and white wine (if used). Bring to a boil.

4. Reduce the heat to medium-low and let it simmer for about 7–10 minutes, stirring occasionally, then pour in the soy sauce and dairy-free cream.

5. Mix the cornstarch and water to make a slurry in a small bowl, then pour it into the pot. Stir to combine and let it simmer for a few more minutes to thicken.

6. Serve the soup in bowls, garnish with parsley, and enjoy! Store leftovers covered in the fridge for 3 days or in the freezer for up to 2 months.

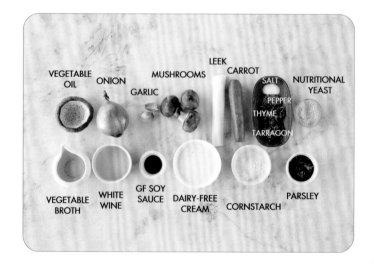

MOROCCAN CHICKPEA STEW

30 minutes, 4 servings

1 Tbsp olive oil

1 large (125 g/4.4 oz) onion, diced

3 garlic cloves, minced

1 can (425 g/15 oz) diced tomatoes

3⅓ cups (800 ml/28.2 oz) vegetable
broth, or more if needed

1 large (375 g/13.2 oz) sweet
potato, peeled and diced

2 medium (400 g/14.1 oz) potatoes,
peeled and diced

2 medium (170 g/6 oz) carrots,
chopped

½ cup (90 g/3.2 oz) red dried lentils,
rinsed

1 can (425 g/15 oz) chickpeas,
drained

1 Tbsp tomato paste

Fresh parsley or cilantro, to garnish

4 dried apricots, finely chopped
(optional)

DRIED SPICES

1 tsp ground cumin

1 tsp ground coriander

1 tsp ground cinnamon

¼ tsp ground turmeric

⅛ tsp ground allspice

Salt and pepper, to taste

Red pepper flakes, to taste

Instructions

1. Heat the olive oil in a large heavy-based pot over medium heat. Add the onion and sauté until soft, about 4–5 minutes. Stir in the fresh garlic and spices and cook until fragrant (1–2 minutes).

2. Add the diced tomatoes and vegetable broth and stir. Then, add the sweet potato, potatoes, carrots, and dried lentils.

3. Stir and bring the mixture to a boil, then reduce the heat to medium-low and let it simmer for 20 minutes.

4. Add the canned chickpeas and tomato paste and cook for a further 5–10 minutes. Optionally, you can also add 4 finely chopped dried apricots.

5. Try it and adjust the seasonings to your liking. If you prefer a thicker stew, add more tomato paste or make a slurry with ½ Tbsp cornstarch + 1 Tbsp water and add it to the stew. However, the stew will thicken naturally over time.

6. Pour the stew into bowls and garnish with fresh parsley or cilantro. Serve with cooked rice or flatbread. Store leftovers covered in the fridge for 3–4 days.

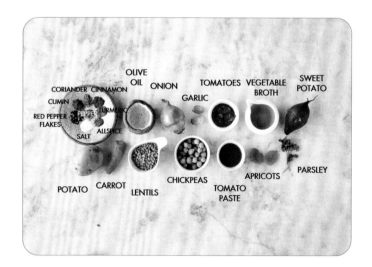

MAIN MEALS

MUSHROOM STROGANOFF

30 minutes, 2 servings

1 Tbsp vegetable oil

1 medium onion, diced

2–3 garlic cloves, minced

300 g (10.6 oz) fresh mushrooms,
  sliced (white button or cremini)

4 Tbsp (50 ml/1.8 oz) white wine (or
  use more vegetable broth)

¾ cup (180 ml/6.3 oz) vegetable
  broth or water

1 Tbsp tamari, GF soy sauce, or
  coconut aminos

1 tsp onion powder

½ tsp garlic powder

½ tsp smoked paprika

1 pinch of red pepper flakes

Salt and black pepper to taste

1 Tbsp nutritional yeast (optional)

¾ cup (180 ml/6.3 oz) plant-based
  milk or cream

2 Tbsp cornstarch or arrowroot flour

Fresh thyme leaves and/or parsley
  (and/or tarragon), chopped

Serve with cooked rice or pasta of
  choice

Instructions

1. Heat oil in a large pan/skillet, add the onion, and sauté for about 5 minutes. Then, add the garlic and sauté for a further minute.

2. Add the mushrooms and sauté over medium heat for 5 minutes.

3. Mix in the white wine (if used), vegetable broth, tamari, and all the spices, including the nutritional yeast. Bring to a boil.

4. Add cornstarch to the plant-based milk or cream and stir to dissolve. Then, pour that into the pan and simmer over medium-low heat for about 10 minutes until the sauce thickens. Taste and adjust any of the seasonings.

5. Finally, add fresh thyme leaves, parsley, and/or tarragon to taste! Enjoy with rice, pasta, or mashed potatoes (page 107). Store leftovers covered in the fridge for 3 days or in the freezer for up to 3 months.

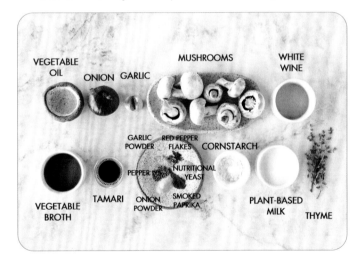

RICE & BEANS

48 minutes, 4 servings

1 ½ cups (300 g/10.6 oz) uncooked
   white rice (jasmine rice or basmati)

1 Tbsp oil or veggie broth

1 medium onion, diced

1 medium red bell pepper, chopped

3–4 garlic cloves, minced

1 tsp ground cumin

1 tsp sweet paprika

1 tsp dried oregano

½ tsp smoked paprika

1 pinch of red pepper flakes

Salt and black pepper to taste

1 ¼ cups (300 g/10.58 oz) salsa
   (or a flavorful tomato sauce)

1 ¼ cups (300 ml/10.58 oz)
   vegetable broth or more,
   depending on rice variety

1 can (425 g/15 oz) kidney beans
   (or pinto beans), drained and rinsed

½ cup (65 g/2.3 oz) green olives,
   halved (optional)

Fresh herbs to garnish (e.g., cilantro
   or parsley)

Instructions

1. Add the rice to a bowl with cold or lukewarm water and let it soak for 30 minutes, then discard the water. Meanwhile, chop the onion, garlic, and bell pepper, and prep the other ingredients.

2. Heat the oil in a large skillet or pot and add the onion and bell pepper. Sauté for about 3 minutes. Stir in the garlic and all spices, and sauté for a further minute.

3. Add the rice, salsa, and veggie broth, and bring the mixture to a boil. Please note that you'll need more vegetable broth and salsa if you're using rice that requires a longer cooking time.

4. Cover the skillet or pot with a lid and let it simmer over low heat for 18 minutes, untouched (do not remove the lid). The cooking time depends on the rice variety (check the package instructions).

5. Turn off the heat, remove the lid and taste it. Adjust seasonings to taste, adding more salt, black pepper, cumin, red pepper flakes, etc., as needed. Stir in the beans and olives (if used), and garnish with fresh herbs (cilantro or parsley) to taste. Store leftovers in the fridge for up to 3 days. Enjoy!

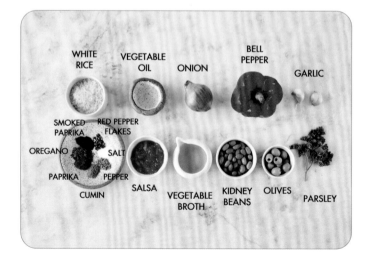

GARLIC NOODLES

25 minutes, 3 servings

227 g (8 oz) noodles, e.g., spaghetti (GF if needed)

2 Tbsp olive oil

6–8 garlic cloves, minced

200 g (7.1 oz) fresh mushrooms, sliced

1 medium bell pepper, thinly sliced

1 Tbsp GF soy sauce, tamari, or coconut aminos

1 Tbsp vegan Worcestershire sauce

½ tsp black pepper

¼ tsp ground cumin

¼ tsp red pepper flakes

1 pinch of turmeric

2 scallions, green part only (chopped)

¼ cup vegan Parmesan cheese

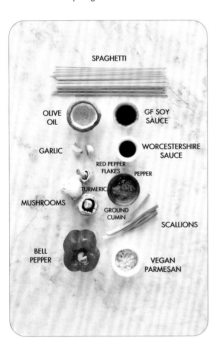

Instructions

1. Cook noodles/pasta of choice according to package directions. I prefer to cook them 1 minute shorter (al dente).

2. Heat the olive oil in a skillet over medium heat and add the garlic. Sauté for 1 minute, stirring frequently, then add the mushrooms and bell pepper.

3. Cook over low-medium heat for about 5 minutes, stirring occasionally, then stir in the soy sauce, vegan Worcestershire sauce, all spices, and scallions.

4. Let simmer for 1 further minute, then finally add the cooked noodles, and stir to combine. Taste it and add more spices and/or soy sauce if desired.

5. Serve in bowls, garnished with vegan Parmesan cheese. Enjoy!

Notes

- **If you prefer a slightly "saucier" dish**: You can save a few spoonfuls of the starchy pasta water to mix into the pan. It will help to make more of a sauce and allow that sauce to better cling to the noodles.

VEGAN MOUSSAKA

60 minutes, 6 servings

BASE

3 large eggplants
1000 g (35.3 oz) potatoes, peeled
Olive oil, to brush
Salt and pepper, to sprinkle

LENTIL MIXTURE

1 Tbsp olive oil
1 large onion, chopped
2 garlic cloves, minced
2 cups (450 g/15.9 oz) passata
    (tomato purée)
1 cup (150 g/5.3 oz) chopped
    tomatoes (canned)
2 bay leaves
1–2 tsp dried thyme
1 tsp oregano
1 tsp paprika
1 tsp coconut sugar or sweetener of
    choice
1 pinch of cinnamon
Salt and pepper to taste
3 cups (600 g/21.2 oz) cooked
    lentils (canned, or cooked from 1
    ½ cups dried lentils)

BÉCHAMEL SAUCE

2 cups (480 ml/16.9 oz) plant-based
    milk
3½ Tbsp (28 g/1 oz) cornstarch or
    arrowroot flour
2 Tbsp nutritional yeast
Salt and pepper to taste
1 pinch of nutmeg
2 Tbsp (28 g/1 oz) vegan butter
Vegan cheese to taste (optional)

Instructions

1. Preheat the oven to 390°F (200°C) and line two baking sheets with parchment paper.

2. Slice each eggplant lengthwise into 4 pieces, and cut the potatoes into ½-inch (1 cm) thick slices. Arrange the slices in a single layer on the baking sheets, brush lightly with some olive oil, and sprinkle with salt and pepper. Bake in the oven for about 20 minutes, or until lightly brown.

3. Meanwhile, heat 1 Tbsp olive oil in a skillet over medium heat. Add the onion and garlic and sauté for 4–5 minutes. Then, add the tomato purée, chopped tomatoes, all spices, salt, and pepper to taste. Finally, add the cooked lentils and let it simmer over low heat for about 5 minutes.

4. For the béchamel sauce, add the plant-based milk to a pan/skillet. Mix in the cornstarch, nutritional yeast, salt, and pepper, and whisk well. Then, add the vegan butter and bring the mixture to a boil.

5. Reduce the heat and simmer over low heat for a few minutes until it thickens, whisking continuously. Remove from the heat.

6. Grease a 13x9-inch (33x23 cm) or larger baking dish and arrange half the potato and eggplant slices on the bottom of the baking dish. Top with the lentil mixture, followed by the remaining potato/eggplant slices. Pour the béchamel sauce over the top and spread it evenly. Add vegan cheese to taste (optional).

7. Bake in the oven for about 30 minutes or until the top is bubbling and golden brown. Garnish with fresh herbs. Enjoy! Store leftovers covered in the fridge for 3–4 days or in the freezer for up to 2 months.

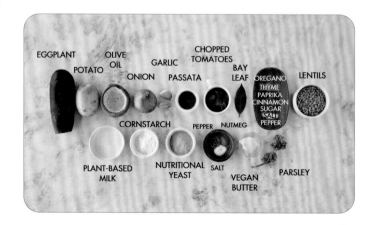

ASIAN STIR-FRY NOODLES

25 minutes, 4 servings

SKILLET

227 g (8 oz) noodles (e.g., linguine or
    rice noodles)

1 Tbsp (sesame) oil

½ heaped Tbsp fresh ginger, grated

3–4 garlic cloves, minced

200 g (7.1 oz) fresh mushrooms,
    chopped or 25 g (0.9 oz) dried
    (rehydrated in water)

1 large carrot, sliced

1 red bell pepper, sliced

1 medium zucchini, sliced

¾ tsp onion powder

½ tsp smoked paprika

Salt and black pepper to taste

Green onion to garnish

Sesame seeds to garnish

SAUCE

⅔ cup (160 ml/5.6 oz) vegetable
    broth or water

3–4 Tbsp tamari, GF soy sauce, or
    coconut aminos

2 Tbsp rice vinegar

2 Tbsp maple syrup (or more to taste)

1 Tbsp cornstarch or arrowroot flour

1 pinch of red pepper flakes
    (optional)

Instructions

1. First, cook the noodles in a pot filled with salted water until al dente (do not overcook them).

2. Meanwhile, heat oil in a skillet or wok and sauté the ginger and garlic over medium heat for about 2 minutes, stirring frequently. Add the mushrooms, carrot, bell pepper, zucchini, and spices. Sauté for about 5 minutes or until the veggies have softened, stirring frequently. You can add a splash of water or veggie broth to avoid burning/sticking.

3. To make the sauce, add all the sauce ingredients (vegetable broth, tamari, rice vinegar, maple syrup, cornstarch, and red pepper flakes) to a medium bowl and whisk well (or to a lidded jar and shake).

4. Pour the sauce into the skillet and bring the mixture to a simmer. Let it simmer for about 1 minute until it thickens.

5. Add the drained noodles and toss to combine. Cook for a further 1–2 minutes, taste it, and adjust any of the seasonings (salt, pepper, tamari, sweetener, etc.) if needed. If you like it creamier, add a few spoonfuls of peanut butter or sunflower seed butter!

6. Garnish with green onions (scallions) and sesame seeds, serve, and enjoy! Store leftovers covered in the fridge for up to 3 days.

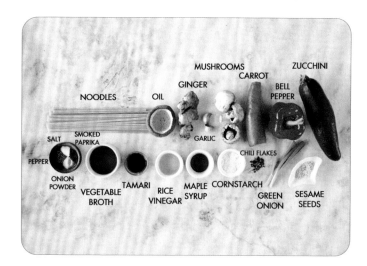

FETTUCCINE ALFREDO

25 minutes, 4 servings

450 g (15.9 oz) cauliflower (small to medium head)

227 g (8 oz) pasta of choice (e.g., fettuccine, gluten-free)

250 g (8.8 oz) fresh mushrooms

3 garlic cloves

2 tsp vegetable oil (divided)

1 cup (240 ml/8.5 oz) vegetable broth or water

¼ cup hemp seeds (shelled) or soaked cashews

1 Tbsp nutritional yeast

1 tsp onion powder

½ tsp garlic powder (optional)

Salt to taste

¼ tsp pepper

1 pinch of smoked paprika and chili powder

Fresh herbs to garnish (e.g., parsley)

Instructions

1. Cut the cauliflower into florets and cook it in salted water for about 10–15 minutes, or until fork-tender. Drain the water.

2. In another pot, cook your pasta of choice according to its package directions.

3. While the cauliflower and pasta cook, slice the mushrooms and mince the garlic.

4. Heat 1 tsp of oil in a skillet and add the garlic. Sauté over medium heat for 2–3 minutes, or until lightly browned.

5. Add the garlic, drained cauliflower, and all the other ingredients (except the pasta, mushrooms, and fresh herbs) to a high-speed blender.

6. Blend on high until smooth (1–2 minutes), then taste it and adjust seasonings if needed.

7. Heat another 1 tsp of oil in a skillet (use the same one you used for the garlic) and add the mushrooms. Sauté for about 3–5 minutes over medium heat and add a pinch of salt and pepper.

8. Pour the Alfredo sauce over the cooked pasta.

9. Add the mushrooms, garnish with fresh herbs (e.g., parsley), and enjoy! Store leftovers covered in the fridge for 3–4 days.

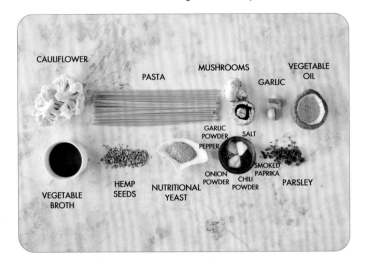

VEGAN MEATLOAF

60 minutes, 8 servings

2 large (400 g / 14.1 oz) potatoes, peeled

1 Tbsp oil

⅔ cup (100 g / 3.5 oz) onion, chopped

3 garlic cloves, minced

2 medium-sized (100 g / 3.5 oz) celery stalks, chopped

½ Tbsp onion powder

¾ tsp salt

½ tsp caraway seeds

½ tsp ground cumin

½ tsp dried thyme

½ tsp smoked paprika

⅓ tsp red pepper flakes

Black pepper to taste

1 Tbsp GF soy sauce, tamari, or coconut aminos

1 Tbsp balsamic vinegar

2 cans (425 g / 15 oz each) black beans or kidney beans, drained and rinsed

2 Tbsp (60 g / 2.1 oz) tomato paste

1 cup (90 g / 3.2 oz) oats, preferably quick oats (see notes)

½ cup (65 g / 2.3 oz) sunflower seeds or nuts of choice

Instructions

1. Chop the potatoes, transfer them to a pot with salted water, and bring to a boil. Cook over medium heat for about 15 minutes or until tender, then drain.

2. Transfer them back to the pot and mash with a potato masher or ricer (don't use a food processor/blender).

3. Preheat the oven to 375°F (190°C).

4. Meanwhile, heat 1 Tbsp oil in a skillet or pan over medium heat and add the chopped onion. Sauté for about 3 minutes, then add the garlic, celery, all the spices, soy sauce, and balsamic vinegar. Cook them for 3–5 minutes, stirring occasionally. Add the beans and then turn off the heat after one minute.

5. Transfer the bean/veggie mixture to the pot with the mashed potatoes and add tomato paste, oats, and sunflower seeds. Then, use the potato masher or your hands to mix everything.

6. Line a 9-inch loaf pan with parchment paper (including an overhang) and put the meatloaf mixture into the pan. Press it down firmly.

7. Bake the vegan loaf for 45–50 minutes, then remove it from the oven and allow it to rest for at least 15 minutes before removing it from the pan (to avoid it falling apart). Then, transfer it to the fridge for at least 3 hours (or overnight) to ensure it firms up before serving.

8. Serve with a maple tomato glaze (see notes below) or mushroom gravy (page 35).

Notes

- **Oats (regular or gluten-free):** You can substitute the oats with buckwheat flour, panko breadcrumbs, or regular breadcrumbs (gluten-free if needed).

- **For a firmer loaf:** You can add 1 Tbsp psyllium husk or use more oats.

- **To serve with the maple tomato glaze:** Combine ¼ cup (56 g) tomato paste, 1½ Tbsp water to thin it, 1 Tbsp each of soy sauce and balsamic vinegar, and ½ Tbsp each of hot sauce and maple syrup. Add onion powder, garlic powder, salt, and pepper to taste. You can add this glaze after baking or for the last 15 minutes of the baking time; then, it will be firmer.

- Store leftovers covered in the fridge for 4 days or in the freezer for up to 3 months.

CURRIED CAULIFLOWER CASSEROLE

40 minutes, 2 servings

CURRY

1 medium cauliflower

1 cup (250 g/8.8 oz) canned diced
 tomatoes

3 garlic cloves, minced

1 inch (2.5 cm) fresh ginger, minced
 or grated

2 tsp curry powder

½ tsp each of salt, onion powder,
 garlic powder, paprika, ground
 cumin

¼ tsp black pepper

CREAM

½ cup (120 ml/4.2 oz) canned
 coconut milk

½ Tbsp cornstarch or tapioca flour/
 starch

1 Tbsp nutritional yeast (optional)

⅓ tsp salt

¼ tsp smoked paprika

OTHER INGREDIENTS

Shredded vegan cheese to taste

Instructions

1. Chop the cauliflower into bite-sized florets, add them to a large pot filled with salted water (or veggie broth) and bring to a boil. Cook for about 10 minutes or until fork-tender (don't overcook it), then drain the water.

2. Preheat the oven to 360°F (180°C). Then, to an oven-safe pan/casserole dish, add the tomatoes, fresh garlic, ginger, and all spices (curry, salt, onion powder, garlic powder, paprika, ground cumin, and black pepper). Stir to combine and add the cooked cauliflower florets.

3. To a medium bowl, add the cream ingredients and whisk well, then pour it over the cauliflower.

4. Bake in the oven for 10 minutes, then stir. Top with vegan cheese and bake for a further 10 minutes. Serve with cooked rice or naan and enjoy! Store leftovers covered in the fridge for 3 days.

VEGAN MAC & CHEESE

25 minutes, 4 servings

½ cup (75 g/2.6 oz) cashews

1 large (200 g/7.1 oz) potato, peeled

1 small (100 g/3.5 oz) carrot, peeled

350 g (12.3 oz) macaroni or pasta of choice (gluten-free if needed)

½ cup (120 ml/4.2 oz) plant-based milk of choice

⅓–½ cup (100 ml/3.5 oz) vegetable broth (or use more plant-based milk)

½ small onion (see notes)

2–3 garlic cloves (see notes)

4 Tbsp nutritional yeast

1 ½ Tbsp tapioca flour/starch (or arrowroot flour)

½ Tbsp lemon juice or lime juice

½–¾ tsp salt (or more to taste)

⅓ tsp black pepper (or to taste)

1 tsp onion powder

Crushed pepper flakes (optional)

Instructions

1. First, soak cashews in hot water for at least 15 minutes until they are soft.

2. Meanwhile, cut the potato and carrot into 1-inch cubes and cook them in salted water for about 10–15 minutes, or until tender (then discard the water).

3. Boil your favorite pasta according to its package directions.

4. Add all the ingredients (except the pasta) to a blender and blend until completely smooth.

5. Pour the sauce into a saucepan and bring it to a boil. Let it simmer for about 1–2 minutes, stirring frequently.

6. Pour it over the cooked pasta and serve immediately. Enjoy!

Notes

- **Onion & garlic:** You can sauté the onion and garlic with a little oil in a skillet for a few minutes to enhance the flavor.

- Store sauce leftovers covered in the fridge for 3 days or in the freezer for up to 3 months.

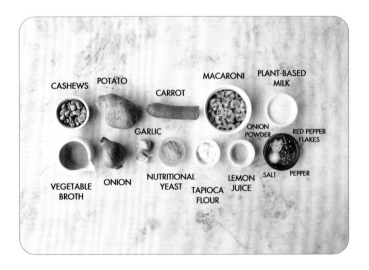

MUJADARA (LENTILS & RICE)

60 minutes, 6 servings

1 cup (180 g/6.3 oz) brown rice

5–5 ½ cups (1250 ml/44 oz) water, divided (see instructions)

1 Tbsp veggie bouillon powder

1 ½ tsp salt, divided

Black pepper to taste

2 bay leaves

1 ½ cups (300 g/10.6 oz) green or brown lentils

2 Tbsp olive oil

5 small-medium (500 g/17.6 oz) onions, sliced

1 tsp ground cumin

Optional: dairy-free yogurt and chopped parsley to taste

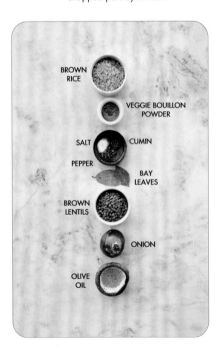

Instructions

1. Soak the brown rice for 20 minutes, then drain.

2. Add the soaked brown rice and 2 ½ cups of water to a large pot and bring it to a boil. Next, stir in the veggie bouillon powder, 1 tsp of salt, black pepper, and 2 bay leaves. Once it starts boiling, reduce the heat, cover the pot with a lid, and let it simmer for 20 minutes.

3. Meanwhile, slice the onions and soak the lentils in a bowl with cold water for 20 minutes. I recommend this step because it cooks the lentils faster and more evenly.

4. Add the drained lentils and 3 cups of water to the rice pot. Stir to combine and cover the pot with a lid. Once it starts boiling, reduce the heat and set the timer to 25 minutes.

5. Meanwhile, heat the oil in a large skillet. Once hot, add the sliced onions. Stir, reduce the heat to medium, and cover the skillet with a lid. Cook the onions for about 10 minutes, then uncover the skillet and stir thoroughly. Add the cumin and ½ tsp of salt and continue to cook the onions without a lid for 5–10 minutes. Increase the heat for crispier results.

6. Once the lentil cooking time is over, check if the rice and lentils are tender. If not, let them simmer for a few more minutes, turn off the heat, and set aside (still covered) for 5 minutes.

7. Remove the bay leaves, then add about ⅔ of the caramelized onions to the lentils and rice pot and reserve the remaining ⅓ for garnish. Serve in bowls, and top with dairy-free yogurt, caramelized onions, and fresh herbs of choice like parsley or cilantro. Enjoy!

8. Store leftovers covered in the fridge for 3 days or in the freezer for up to 3 months.

MUSHROOM BOURGUIGNON

50 minutes, 3 servings

28 g (1 oz) dried mushrooms or 280
  g (10 oz) fresh sliced mushrooms

1 Tbsp oil

½ large onion, diced

2 small/medium (140 g/4.9 oz)
  carrots, chopped

⅔ cup (100 g/3.5 oz) peas, frozen

3 garlic cloves, minced

¾ Tbsp fresh thyme or 1 tsp dried
  thyme

1 tsp onion powder

¾ tsp salt (or to taste)

¼ tsp black pepper (or to taste)

¼ tsp smoked paprika

⅓ cup (80 ml/2.8 oz) red wine (or
  use more vegetable broth)

½ Tbsp tamari, GF soy sauce, or
  coconut aminos

¾ cup (180 ml/6.3 oz) vegetable
  broth + ¼ cup more if needed

¼ cup (60 ml/2.1 oz) plant-based
  milk

¾ Tbsp cornstarch or arrowroot flour

Instructions

1. Soak the dried mushrooms in warm water for 15–20 minutes, then drain. Skip this step if using fresh mushrooms.

2. Heat oil in a pan over medium heat. Add the onion and sauté for 4–5 minutes. Then, add the mushrooms, carrot, peas, garlic, thyme, and spices. Sauté for a minute, stirring frequently.

3. Add the red wine (or extra vegetable broth) and cook for about 2 minutes. Then, add the tamari (or soy sauce) and vegetable broth.

4. Let it simmer over medium-low heat with a lid on for 10–12 minutes, or until the carrots and peas have softened.

5. Combine plant-based milk and cornstarch in a bowl and whisk until there are no lumps. Add the mixture to the pan and stir well. Let it simmer for a few more minutes until it thickens.

6. Taste and adjust any of the seasonings (salt, pepper, spices) if needed. Serve over mashed potatoes (page 107) and enjoy! Store leftovers covered in the fridge for up to 3 days.

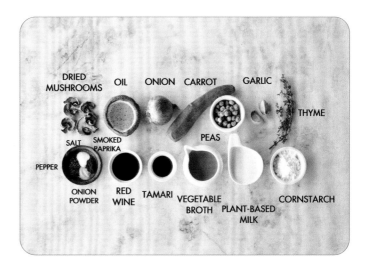

VEGAN SHEPHERD'S PIE

50 minutes, 4 servings

MASHED POTATOES

1000 g (35.3 oz) potatoes

2 Tbsp vegan butter or vegetable oil

¼ cup (60 ml/2.1 oz) plant-based
  milk

Nutmeg, black pepper, and salt to
  taste

FILLING

½ Tbsp vegetable oil

1 onion, diced

2 garlic cloves, minced

2 medium carrots, diced

1 celery stalk, diced

1 tsp onion powder

1 tsp dried thyme (or 2 tsp fresh)

½ tsp dried rosemary (or tarragon)

½ tsp coconut sugar or sweetener of
  choice

Salt and pepper to taste

2 Tbsp tomato paste

2 Tbsp GF soy sauce or coconut
  aminos

1 Tbsp balsamic vinegar

2 cups (400 g/14.1 oz) cooked
  lentils (cooked from dry or use
  canned)

½ cup (80 g/2.8 oz) corn, fresh,
  frozen, or canned

½ cup peas (frozen or canned)

¼ cup (60 ml/2.1 oz) vegetable stock

¼ cup (60 ml/2.1 oz) red wine or
  more veggie stock

Instructions

1. Peel and chop the potatoes, transfer them to a pot with salted water, and bring to a boil. Cook over medium heat for about 15 minutes or until tender, then drain.

2. Transfer the potatoes back to the pot with vegan butter, plant-based milk, nutmeg, black pepper, and salt to taste. Mash with a potato masher (don't use a food processor/blender).

3. Meanwhile, heat oil in a skillet over medium heat, add the onion, garlic, carrot, celery, and all spices, and sauté them for about 3 minutes. Then, add the tomato paste, soy sauce, and balsamic vinegar. Stir to combine.

4. Add the cooked lentils, corn, peas, red wine, and vegetable stock. Bring to a boil and let it simmer for about 5–7 minutes, or until slightly reduced.

5. Preheat the oven to 390°F (200°C).

6. Spoon the lentil mixture into a baking dish (I use a square 9-inch pan). Spoon the mashed potatoes over the lentil mixture and spread it evenly.

7. Bake for 15 minutes, then broil for a few minutes until golden brown on top.

8. Garnish with fresh herbs and enjoy! Store leftovers covered in the fridge for up to 4 days.

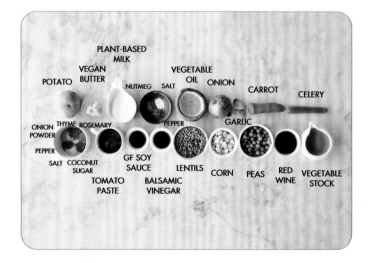

SPICY NOODLES

25 minutes, 4 servings

227 g (8 oz) rice noodles (or noodles
  of choice)

1 Tbsp oil

3–4 garlic cloves, minced

1 Tbsp ginger fresh, grated

1 hot red chili pepper, minced

2 sweet red peppers, chopped

3 spring onions, chopped

Salt and black pepper to taste

¼ tsp smoked paprika

3 Tbsp (60 g/2.1 oz) tomato paste

1 Tbsp Sriracha (or less/more to
  taste)

Sesame seeds, to garnish

SAUCE

⅔ cup (160 ml/5.6 oz) vegetable
  broth or water

2–3 Tbsp GF dark soy sauce or
  coconut aminos

1 Tbsp rice vinegar

1 Tbsp maple syrup (or more to taste)

½ Tbsp cornstarch or arrowroot flour

½ tsp sesame oil

Red pepper flakes to taste

Instructions

1. Cook rice noodles (or your favorite noodles) in salted water until al
    dente, then drain.

2. Meanwhile, heat oil in a skillet and sauté the garlic and ginger over
    medium heat for about 1 minute, stirring frequently. Add the chili
    pepper, red sweet pepper, the whites of the spring onions, salt, pepper,
    and smoked paprika. Sauté for about 4 minutes, stirring frequently.
    Then, stir in tomato paste and Sriracha.

3. To make the sauce, add the sauce ingredients (vegetable broth, dark
    soy sauce, rice vinegar, maple syrup, cornstarch, sesame oil, and red
    pepper flakes) to a medium bowl or jar and whisk.

4. Pour the sauce into the pan and bring to a simmer. Let it simmer for
    about 1 minute to thicken.

5. Add the drained noodles and toss to combine with the sauce. Cook for
    a further minute, then taste it and adjust any of the seasonings if needed.

6. Garnish with the greens of the spring onions and sesame seeds, serve,
    and enjoy! Store leftovers covered in the fridge for up to 3 days.

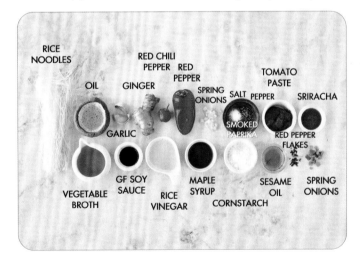

CHILI SIN CARNE

45 minutes, 4 servings

2 tsp oil of choice for frying

1 medium onion, chopped

1 green pepper, chopped

4 garlic cloves, minced

5–6 medium diced fresh tomatoes or
 use 1 (570 g/20 oz) can

1 medium carrot, grated

5 Tbsp tomato paste

2 cups (480 ml/16.9 oz) water or
 vegetable broth

4 cups (650 g/22.9 oz) cooked
 (canned) beans of choice, drained
 and rinsed

2 tsp coconut sugar or sweetener
 of choice

1 tsp ground cumin

1 tsp onion powder

1 tsp garlic powder

¾ tsp salt (or less if you use
 vegetable broth)

½ tsp black pepper

¼ tsp smoked paprika

¼ tsp cayenne pepper

1–2 hot red chili peppers

Instructions

1. Heat oil in a large pan or pot over medium heat. Then sauté the onion and pepper for about 5 minutes, add the garlic, and sauté for an additional 1–2 minutes, stirring occasionally.

2. Add the tomatoes and sauté for a further 3–5 minutes.

3. Now add all remaining ingredients, increase the heat, and let simmer for about 30 minutes or longer (for more developed flavor), stirring occasionally. Add more water or vegetable broth if the chili gets too thick.

4. **Recommended step:** Pour 1–1 ½ cups of the chili into a different pot. Blend this part using an immersion blender (or regular blender) until smooth. Then pour the blended chili back into the large pot and stir to combine.

5. Serve with rice, pasta, potatoes, or flatbread. Garnish with fresh cilantro or parsley. Store leftovers covered in the fridge for 4–5 days or in the freezer for up to 3 months.

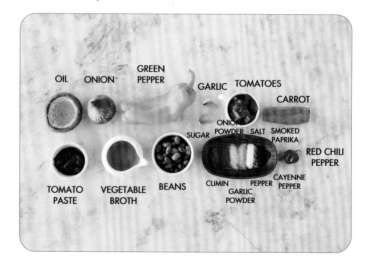

MUSHROOM RISOTTO

35 minutes, 4 servings

2 Tbsp coconut oil, divided

1 medium onion, diced (divided)

2 large garlic cloves, minced (divided)

½ cup (120 g/4.2 oz) risotto rice

¼ cup (60 ml/2.1 oz) white wine (or use more broth)

1 ¼ cup (300 ml/10.6 oz) vegetable broth, heated on the stove

200 g (7.1 oz) fresh mushrooms, sliced

1 cup (150 g/5.3 oz) chickpeas, canned

1 Tbsp balsamic vinegar

1 Tbsp GF soy sauce, tamari, or coconut aminos

½ cup (120 ml/4.2 oz) canned coconut milk

Nutritional yeast, to garnish

Black pepper, salt, red pepper flakes, and fresh parsley to taste

Instructions

1. Heat 1 Tbsp coconut oil in a skillet/frying pan, stir in ½ of the diced onion and 1 large clove of minced garlic, and sauté for a few minutes over medium heat.

2. Add the rice and stir for about 1 minute until it's opaque. Then pour in the wine, stirring constantly until the wine has absorbed.

3. Add ½ cup vegetable broth and cook over low heat until the broth has been absorbed. Stir frequently and add more broth, ¼ cup at a time, until the liquid has absorbed and the risotto is al dente and creamy (about 15 minutes).

4. In a different skillet/frying pan, heat the remaining 1 Tbsp coconut oil and stir in the remaining diced onion and minced garlic. Sauté for a few minutes over medium heat.

5. Add the mushrooms and chickpeas and sauté for 3–5 minutes. Then, add the balsamic vinegar, soy sauce, and coconut milk, and let it simmer for 5 minutes, stirring occasionally. Season with black pepper, salt, red pepper flakes, and fresh parsley to taste.

6. Finally, combine the mushroom/chickpea mixture with the cooked risotto rice, stir in the nutritional yeast flakes, and enjoy! Store leftovers covered in the fridge for up to 3 days.

LENTIL BOLOGNESE

40 minutes, 4 servings

1 cup (200 g/7.1 oz) dried lentils of
   your choice (I used brown), soaked

1 Tbsp oil

1 medium onion, finely diced

1 medium (52 g/1.8 oz) celery stalk,
   finely diced (½ cup)

280 g (10 oz) fresh mushrooms, finely
   diced (or 28 g/1 oz dried)

2 medium (200 g/7.1 oz) carrots,
   finely grated

4 garlic cloves, minced or crushed

1 tsp coconut sugar or sweetener of
   choice

2 tsp Italian seasoning, or use 1 tsp
   each of dried oregano and basil

1 tsp onion powder

Salt, black pepper, and red pepper
   flakes to taste

⅓ cup (80 ml/2.8 oz) red wine or
   use more vegetable broth

3 cups (750 g/26.5 oz) crushed
   tomatoes (or marinara sauce or
   tomato sauce)

2 cups (480 ml/16.9 oz) vegetable
   broth

1 bay leaf

227 g (8 oz) spaghetti, gluten-free if
   needed (or pasta of choice)

1 Tbsp GF soy sauce, tamari, or
   coconut aminos

1 Tbsp balsamic vinegar

½ cup (120 ml/4.2 oz) plant-based
   milk

1 tsp cornstarch or arrowroot flour

Vegan Parmesan or nutritional yeast
   to garnish (optional)

Instructions

1. I recommend soaking the lentils in lukewarm water for 20 minutes if you are using green or brown lentils (not red lentils). The lentils will cook faster and are better digested when soaked.

2. Heat oil in a pan or pot over medium heat. Add the onion, celery, mushrooms, and carrots, and sauté for 3–4 minutes. Stir in the garlic, sweetener, and all spices, and sauté for a further minute, stirring frequently.

3. Add the red wine (or vegetable broth), crushed tomatoes, vegetable broth, bay leaf, and the drained lentils. Stir to combine.

4. Bring to a boil and let it simmer for 20 minutes or until the lentils are tender (depending on the variety, it can take shorter or longer).

5. Meanwhile, cook your favorite pasta (e.g., spaghetti) according to its package directions.

6. Add soy sauce and balsamic vinegar. Then, mix the plant-based milk and cornstarch in a small bowl to make a "slurry" and add it to the pan. Simmer until it thickens.

7. Taste and adjust seasonings (salt, pepper, spices) to your liking. Also, add more vegetable broth if needed.

8. Serve the lentil Bolognese in bowls over pasta and sprinkle vegan Parmesan over the top (optional). Enjoy! Store the Bolognese sauce leftovers covered in the fridge for up to 4 days or freeze for up to 3 months.

SNACKS & LIGHT MEALS

VEGETABLE ZUCCHINI FRITTERS

35 minutes, 6 fritters

1 large (375 g/13.2 oz) zucchini

2 medium (300 g/10.6 oz) potatoes
   (Yukon Gold or Russet)

1 medium (80 g/2.8 oz) carrot

½ tsp garlic powder

½ tsp onion powder

½ tsp chili powder

½ tsp ground cumin

½ tsp paprika powder

½ tsp salt

Black pepper to taste

½ cup (50 g/1.8 oz) chickpea flour

Instructions

1. Grate the zucchini, potatoes, and carrot, and squeeze out as much liquid as possible from the veggies using a nut milk bag, cheesecloth, or a clean kitchen towel.

2. Add the veggies to a skillet and stir in all the spices. Cook over medium-low heat with a lid for about 10 minutes, stirring occasionally, then turn off the heat.

3. Add in the chickpea flour and stir with a spatula to combine. Let the mixture cool, until you can touch it.

4. Shape the mixture into 6 patties using your hands. Then, you can choose between the following three cooking methods:

   - **Pan-Fry:** Heat some oil in a frying pan and place 3–4 patties in it (or as many that will fit). Sauté on both sides until crispy (about 4–5 minutes per side).

   - **Air-Fry:** Cook at 380°F (193°C) for 15 minutes in your air fryer (flip after 10 minutes). I recommend spraying the basket of your air fryer with a little oil before adding the patties, otherwise, they may stick.

   - **Bake:** Preheat the oven to 400°F (205°C) and bake the patties for 35–40 minutes on a lined baking sheet (flipping after 20–25 minutes). For a crispier result, I recommend spraying the patties with a bit of oil before baking and after flipping. Enjoy!

STUFFED POTATO CAKES

50 minutes, 8 potato cakes

DOUGH

1000 g (35.3 oz) Yukon Gold or
   Russet potatoes (see notes)
Salt, pepper, and nutmeg to taste
½ cup (80 g/2.8 oz) white rice flour
   (or regular flour, if not GF)
⅓ cup (40 g/1.4 oz) cornstarch or
   tapioca flour/starch

FILLING

1 onion, chopped
250 g (8.8 oz) fresh mushrooms, sliced
2 garlic cloves, minced
1 bell pepper, diced
½ zucchini, diced
Salt and pepper to taste
1 tsp Italian spice blend
1 tsp onion powder
1 tsp garlic powder
½ tsp cumin
¼ tsp red pepper flakes

ADDITIONAL INGREDIENTS

Oil for frying
Vegan cheese to taste (optional)

Instructions

Dough

1. Peel the potatoes, cut them into 2-inch pieces, and cook them in salted water for 20 minutes, or until tender but not mushy.

2. Season with salt, pepper, and nutmeg, and mash them with a potato masher or ricer. (Please do not use a food processor, or the mashed potatoes will be gloopy.)

3. Allow the mashed potatoes to cool (meanwhile, prepare the filling), then add the flour and cornstarch and mix well with a spoon or your hands.

Filling

1. Sauté the onion in a pan with a bit of oil for about 3–4 minutes, then add the mushrooms, garlic, diced peppers, and zucchini. Sauté everything for a couple of minutes, then season them with salt, pepper, and the spice mix.

2. Divide the dough into 8 parts (around ½ cup or 120 g each). Shape them into balls, make a well in the middle, and add about 1 ½ tablespoons of the filling. You can also add some vegan cheese (for this, I used the vegan cheese sauce on page 31). Carefully "seal" the balls with more dough and flatten them slightly to make them look like thick pancakes/patties.

3. Heat approximately 2 tablespoons of oil in a pan and fry the potato cakes over medium heat until golden brown on both sides. They will be crisp on the outside and soft in the middle. If you want them to be slightly crunchier, you can bake them for an additional 20 minutes at 375ºF (190ºC) in the oven. Enjoy!

Notes

• If the potatoes are very floury, use less rice flour (e.g., just ¼ cup). The dough shouldn't be too dry or crumbly. If it's too sticky, add more flour.

• Store leftovers covered in the fridge for up to 4 days.

CAULIFLOWER PATTIES

30 minutes, 8–10 patties

WET INGREDIENTS

½ small (250 g/8.8 oz) cauliflower
    head, cut into small florets

1 can (425 g/15 oz) chickpeas,
    drained and rinsed

2 Tbsp parsley, finely chopped

2 garlic cloves, minced

Oil for frying

DRY INGREDIENTS

½ heaped cup (60 g/2.1 oz)
    chickpea flour

1½ Tbsp ground flax seeds

1 tsp onion powder

½ tsp cumin ground

Salt and pepper to taste

Instructions

1. Cook the cauliflower florets in salted water until tender (about 10–15 minutes), then discard the water.

2. Meanwhile, combine all dry ingredients in a bowl and set aside.

3. Pulse all the wet ingredients (except the oil) in a food processor until combined. (Don't over-process, though. There should still be texture, not a paste.)

4. Add the wet ingredients to the bowl of dry ingredients and combine with your hands.

5. Form 8–10 patties and fry them with a little oil in a large skillet on both sides (about 5 minutes each) until golden brown.

6. Serve with a dip of your choice. Check my dip recipes on page 29.

Notes

- You can add a little grated vegan cheese and some chopped veggies to the batter to make the patties tastier.

- Store leftovers covered in the fridge for up to 4 days.

LOW-CARB CRACKERS

20 minutes, 60 small crackers

1 cup (120 g/4.2 oz) ground
   sunflower seeds (or almond flour)

4 tsp nutritional yeast (or more to taste)

2 tsp psyllium husk powder (see notes)

1–2 tsp Italian seasoning

¾–1 tsp salt

1 tsp garlic powder

1 tsp onion powder

½ tsp smoked paprika

¼ cup (56 ml/2 oz) dairy-free milk

GROUND
SUNFLOWER SEEDS

NUTRITIONAL
YEAST

PSYLLIUM HUSK
POWDER

ITALIAN
SEASONING

ONION
POWDER

GARLIC
POWDER

SMOKED
PAPRIKA

SALT

DAIRY-FREE
MILK

Instructions

1. Preheat the oven to 350°F (177°C).

2. Add all the ingredients (except the dairy-free milk) to a medium-sized bowl and stir with a spoon (or process in a food processor).

3. Add the dairy-free milk and mix again, and let the dough rest for 1–2 minutes. Then use your hands to knead the dough for a few seconds until it's smooth.

4. Shape it into a dough ball and place it between two sheets of parchment paper. Flatten it with your hand, then roll it out with a rolling pin into a rectangle about 1⁄16 inch (0.2 cm) thick. Peel off the top layer of parchment paper.

5. You can now optionally sprinkle more seeds (chia, flax, pumpkin, sunflower, etc.) on top, pressing them down slightly. Cut the dough (using a knife or pizza cutter) into small squares.

6. Transfer the parchment paper to a baking sheet and bake for 10–15 minutes or until slightly golden brown around the edges. The baking time depends on how thin you rolled out the dough, so check after 10 minutes to see if the edges are already browning. Leave the crackers in the oven for a few more minutes if you want them crispier. They will crisp up further as they cool.

7. Enjoy! Store leftover crackers covered at room temp for 6–7 days or in the freezer for up to 2 months.

Notes

- **Sunflower seeds:** I grind whole sunflower seeds in an electric coffee/spice grinder until I get a fine flour. You can also use store-bought sunflower seed flour instead, though.

- **Psyllium husk:** I use psyllium husk powder, but you can use 4 teaspoons of whole psyllium husk. Xanthan gum might work too.

BLACK BEAN BURGER

30 minutes, 4 servings

BURGER

3 Tbsp ground chia seeds + ¼ cup
(60 ml/2.1 oz) water

1 can (425 g/15 oz) black beans,
drained and rinsed

⅔ cup (60 g/2.1 oz) quick oats
(gluten-free if needed)

½ cup (65 g/2.3 oz) sunflower seeds
(see notes)

1 heaped Tbsp (30 g/1.1 oz)
tomato paste

1½ Tbsp GF soy sauce, tamari, or
coconut aminos

3 garlic cloves, minced

½ large (65 g/2.3 oz) onion, chopped

2 tsp onion powder

2 tsp smoked paprika

½ tsp ground cumin

¼ tsp red pepper flakes (or less/
more to taste)

¾ tsp salt (or less/more to taste)

Black pepper to taste

3 Tbsp fresh parsley, finely chopped

OTHER INGREDIENTS

Oil for frying

Vegan barbecue sauce (optional)

4 burger buns, regular or gluten-free

Fresh veggies of choice (e.g.,
tomatoes, lettuce, onion, cucumber)

Vegan cheese

Dressing of choice

Instructions

1. Mix 3 Tbsp of ground chia seeds with ¼ cup of water in a small bowl and set that aside for 5 minutes to thicken. If you don't have ground chia seeds, blend whole chia seeds in an electric spice/coffee grinder or blender for a few seconds.

2. Meanwhile, rinse the canned beans well, drain them, and pat dry.

3. Pulse the oats and the sunflower seeds in a food processor or blender. Then, add the remaining burger ingredients to the food processor and process again. Don't over-process, to maintain some texture.

4. Form 4 burger patties with your hands. If the mixture is too sticky, add more oats. If it's too dry, add a little water.

5. Heat some oil in a large frying pan and add the 4 burger patties. Fry them on both sides until they firm up. It will take about 12–15 minutes in total. **Tip:** Brush the burgers with vegan barbecue sauce or Sriracha after flipping for even more delicious flavor!

6. Assemble the burgers in burger buns with fresh ingredients such as onion rings, tomato slices, cucumber slices, fresh lettuce leaves, and avocado (guacamole). I also added my vegan cheese sauce (page 31).

Notes

• These black bean burgers are firm on the outside but soft in the middle. If you want them to be firmer inside, first pan-fry the burger patties and then bake them at 375°F (ca. 190°C) for about 15 minutes.

• **Sunflower seeds:** You can use nuts such as walnuts or cashews instead of sunflower seeds.

• Store covered in the fridge for up to 3 days or freeze for up to 3 months.

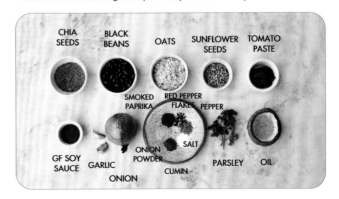

CRISPY FALAFEL

45 minutes, 25 balls

2 cups (400 g / 14.1 oz) dried
    chickpeas (**not** cooked)

5 garlic cloves, chopped

1 small onion, chopped

1 cup parsley leaves, chopped

½ cup cilantro leaves, chopped

2 tsp ground coriander

2 tsp ground cumin

1½ tsp salt

1 tsp black pepper

Red pepper flakes or cayenne
    pepper to taste

1 tsp baking powder
    (optional, see notes)

Cooking spray

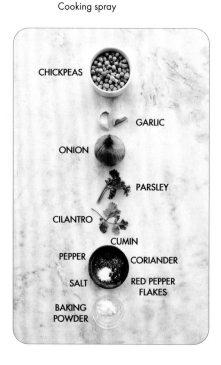

Instructions

1. The day before making the falafel, leave the dried chickpeas to soak in a bowl covered with at least 3 inches (7 cm) of water (or more) for 18–24 hours. Then, drain the chickpeas and use a paper towel to pat them dry.

2. Transfer the chickpeas and all the other ingredients to a large food processor (if you have a smaller one, simply work in batches). Process everything for about 20 seconds, then scrape down the sides of the food processor and blend again. Do this a few times until the mixture is well combined but not mushy.

3. Refrigerate the falafel mixture in the food processor bowl for 45–60 minutes (or longer).

4. Then, use an ice cream scoop to scoop the falafel mixture and shape it with your hands to form a ball (or make a patty/disk if you wish). Repeat this with the remaining falafel mixture.

5. Use the cooking spray to spray the falafel balls lightly. Also, spray the basket of your air fryer to avoid sticking. Heat the air fryer to 375°F (190°C) and set the timer to 15 minutes. Cook the falafel balls in the air fryer, making sure there's space between each one, and flip them after 10 minutes. They should be crispy and slightly brown on the outside. You might need to fry them in batches if necessary.

6. Serve hot on their own, or assemble the falafels in pita bread with tahini, lettuce, tomato, and cucumbers. Enjoy!

Notes

*   **Flour:** I didn't add flour to the falafel mixture because it held well and didn't require a binder. However, if you notice that your mixture needs a binder, add 2 tablespoons of chickpea flour (or regular flour or cornstarch) and a little water if the mixture is too dry.

*   **Baking powder:** This will result in slightly lighter and airier, more tender falafel. Add it just before frying (don't add it to the mixture before chilling it in the fridge or freezing).

*   **Oven-baked falafel:** It's better to shape the falafel mixture into patties if you want to oven-bake them. Bake at 375°F (190°C) for about 25 minutes, flipping halfway through. I also recommend spraying them with oil (cooking spray) before baking and after flipping, as they will turn out crispier.

BLACK BEAN QUESADILLAS

30 minutes, 6 servings

1 Tbsp oil, divided

1 Tbsp GF soy sauce, tamari, or
   coconut aminos

½ onion, chopped

2 garlic cloves, minced

1 bell pepper, chopped

125 g (4.4 oz) fresh mushrooms,
   sliced

½ cup (80 g/2.8 oz) corn, fresh,
   frozen, or canned

⅔ cup (120 g/4.2 oz) black beans,
   cooked from dry or canned

1 tsp onion powder

½ tsp cumin powder

½ tsp (ground) oregano

¼ tsp smoked paprika

⅓ tsp red pepper flakes (optional)

Salt and pepper to taste

1 batch of vegan cheese sauce
   (page 31) or another vegan cheese

6 tortillas (I use homemade GF,
   (page 52)

Instructions

1. Heat ½ Tbsp oil in a pan and add 1 Tbsp soy sauce with the onion, garlic, pepper, and mushrooms. Sauté over medium heat for 3–4 minutes. Then add the corn, black beans, and all spices, and sauté for 3–4 minutes.

2. Make a batch of my vegan cheese sauce (page 31) and spread some of it in an even layer over 1 tortilla.

3. Add a layer of the veggie mixture (about 2–4 Tbsp) and place another tortilla on top.

4. Transfer to a (lightly oiled) skillet and cook for about 2–3 minutes. Brush the top lightly with some oil, flip, and cook from the other side until both sides are nicely browned and toasty.

5. Repeat all the steps for the remaining tortillas. Cut into 4 pieces and enjoy it hot!

Notes

- **Vegan cheese sauce:** I add 1 teaspoon of psyllium husk powder, which helps make the sauce thicker and "glue" the tortillas together.

VEGETABLE TAQUITOS

45 minutes, 10 taquitos

2 medium-large (400 g/14.1 oz)
    potatoes, peeled and chopped

½ Tbsp oil

½ medium-large onion, chopped

1 medium (140 g/4.9 oz) carrot,
    grated or finely diced

3 garlic cloves, minced

1 tsp curry powder

1 tsp onion powder

½ tsp ground cumin

¼ tsp ground nutmeg

¾–1 tsp salt (or less/more to taste)

¼ tsp smoked paprika

Red pepper flakes to taste

Black pepper to taste

¼ cup (60 ml/2.1 oz)
    vegetable broth

1 cup (180 g/6.3 oz) peas, frozen
    or canned

140 g (4.9 oz) vegan cheese
    of choice

8–10 small/medium tortillas (see notes)

Optional: taco seasoning to sprinkle
    on top of taquitos

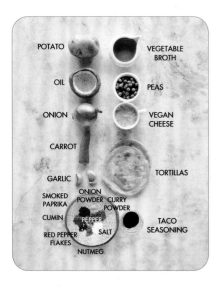

Instructions

1. Peel and chop the potatoes and cook them in a pot of salted boiling water until fork-tender (about 12–15 minutes). Drain the water and mash the potatoes with a potato masher/ricer. Add a splash of plant-based milk for a creamier mash, then set aside.

2. Heat oil in a pan/skillet over medium-high heat and add the chopped onion. Sauté for 3 minutes, stirring frequently, then add the grated carrot, minced garlic, and all the spices, and sauté for a further minute.

3. Pour in the vegetable broth and add the peas (frozen), put the lid on, and cook for a few minutes until the carrot is softened. If using canned peas, drain and rinse them and add in the next step (not now). Turn off the heat.

4. Add the mashed potatoes and vegan cheese (store-bought grated vegan cheese, cream cheese, or my vegan cheese sauce from page 31). Use a fork or a potato masher to combine everything.

5. Taste the veggie mixture and adjust the seasonings accordingly. If you want it spicier, add more red pepper flakes to taste.

6. Preheat the oven to 410°F (210°C) and line a large baking sheet with parchment paper.

7. Place 2–3 Tbsp of the filling onto each tortilla and roll them up tightly. Place every tortilla seam-side down on the baking sheet, next to each other.

8. Brush with a little vegetable oil (to make them crispier) and sprinkle with taco seasoning.

9. Bake in the oven for 17–20 minutes, or until they are golden brown and crispy. For even crispier tops, broil them for a few minutes.

10. Serve with salsa, sour cream, vegan queso, or guacamole. Enjoy!

Notes

- **Tortillas:** I use homemade gluten-free tortillas (page 52).

- Store leftovers covered in the fridge for up to 3 days or freeze in a zip-top bag for up to 2 months.

BAKED SPINACH TACOS

40 minutes, 9 tacos

2 cups (360 g/12.7 oz) cooked rice
 (about ⅔–1 cup uncooked rice)

9 small spinach tortillas (5-inch
 diameter) (page 56)

½ Tbsp oil

1 small/medium onion, diced

¾ cup (100 g/3.5 oz) canned
 mushrooms (or use fresh)

½ bell pepper, chopped

2 garlic cloves, minced

½ tsp onion powder

½ tsp ground cumin

½ tsp paprika

¼ tsp smoked paprika

¼ tsp ground ginger (optional)

¼ tsp black pepper (or more to taste)

Salt to taste

1 Tbsp balsamic vinegar

1 Tbsp GF soy sauce, tamari, or
 coconut aminos

4 Tbsp plant-based milk

⅓ cup (80 g/2.8 oz) passata

2 Tbsp hot sauce (or use less/more
 to taste)

1 can (425 g/15 oz) kidney beans or
 black beans, drained and rinsed

1 batch of vegan cheese sauce
 (page 31, or use store-bought
 vegan cheese)

Instructions

1. Cook rice according to package directions and prepare the spinach tortillas (page 56) or use store-bought tortillas.

2. Meanwhile, heat oil in a pan/skillet over medium heat and add the onion, mushrooms, and bell pepper.

3. Sauté for 3–5 minutes, then add the garlic and sauté for a further minute. Stir occasionally.

4. Add the spices, balsamic vinegar, soy sauce, plant-based milk, passata, and hot sauce. Stir and let it simmer for about 3 minutes.

5. Add cooked rice and beans, stir, and turn off the heat. Taste and adjust any seasonings accordingly.

6. Preheat the oven to 410°F (210°C) and line a baking sheet with parchment paper.

7. Make one batch of the vegan cheese sauce (page 31) or use store-bought vegan cheese. Then add about 2 Tbsp of the rice filling to one side of the tortilla with 1 Tbsp of the vegan cheese sauce. Fold the other side over the filling and press it slightly to close. Repeat with the remaining tortillas.

8. Transfer all the tortillas onto the baking sheet. Bake in the oven for 10–15 minutes, or until crispy. Enjoy hot!

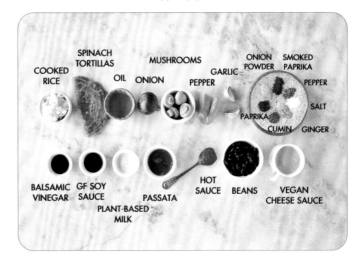

SPINACH PASTA SAUCE

10 minutes, 2 servings

90 g (3.2 oz) fresh spinach

1 handful of fresh basil

1 cup (240 ml/8.5 oz) lite canned
coconut milk (or any other dairy-
free milk)

2 Tbsp nutritional yeast

1 Tbsp cornstarch or potato starch

2 garlic cloves

1 tsp onion powder

⅓–½ tsp salt (or to taste)

Black pepper to taste

1 pinch of nutmeg

Instructions

1. Blend all the ingredients in a blender until completely smooth.

2. Transfer the mixture to a saucepan and bring it to a boil, stirring regularly.

3. Let it simmer for 1–2 minutes and stir frequently.

4. Serve with cooked pasta (or grains/potatoes) and enjoy. Store sauce leftovers covered in the fridge for 3–4 days.

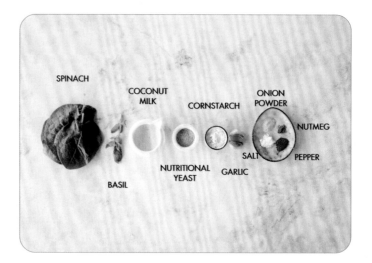

VEGAN GRILLED CHEESE

25 minutes, 4 servings

1 large carrot

1 ½ Tbsp oil, divided

4–5 Tbsp vegetable broth or water

1 onion, diced

1 tsp onion powder

½ tsp garlic powder

⅓ tsp smoked paprika

½ tsp Italian seasoning

Salt and black pepper to taste

1 pinch of cayenne pepper (optional)

½ Tbsp GF soy sauce, tamari, or
   coconut aminos

½ Tbsp balsamic vinegar

56 g (2 oz) fresh baby spinach

4 slices sandwich bread, gluten-free
   if needed

1 batch of vegan cheese sauce
(page 31) or store-bought vegan
   cheese

Instructions

Carrot

1. Slice one large carrot lengthwise into strips (about ¼-inch or 0.6 cm thick). Meanwhile, heat ½ Tbsp oil in a skillet.

2. Once hot, add the carrot slices and sprinkle with salt and sauté. Add 4–5 Tbsp of vegetable broth or water after a few minutes to avoid burning.

3. Cook with the lid on over medium heat until tender, about 12–15 minutes (adding more broth/water if needed). Flip halfway through.

Spinach/Onion Mixture

1. Meanwhile, heat ½ Tbsp oil in a different pan and add the diced onion. Sauté for 4–5 minutes or until nicely browned.

2. Add all the spices, soy sauce, balsamic vinegar, and spinach. Turn off the heat after 60 seconds and set the pan aside.

Assembly

1. Brush or drizzle 4 slices of bread with oil and heat them up in a pan or on the grill for a few minutes.

2. Prepare the vegan cheese sauce (page 31), or skip this step if using store-bought vegan cheese.

3. Top the 2 slices of bread with 1 heaped Tbsp of the vegan cheese sauce, followed by the spinach and onion mixture. Then add the carrot slices and another layer of vegan cheese sauce.

4. Finally, top with the other slice of bread and cook over medium heat in a skillet or on the grill for 2–3 minutes on both sides, until golden brown. Enjoy!

SWEET & SOUR CHICKPEAS

10 minutes, 2 servings

4 Tbsp tomato paste

5 Tbsp (75 ml/2.6 oz) orange juice

½ Tbsp cornstarch or arrowroot flour

½ cup (120 ml/4.2 oz) water

1 tsp veggie bouillon powder

1 Tbsp tamari or coconut aminos

2–3 tsp coconut sugar or sweetener
of choice

1 tsp hot sauce

½ Tbsp oil

2 garlic cloves, minced

1 can (425 g/15 oz) chickpeas,
drained and rinsed

½ Tbsp peanut butter or sunflower
seed butter

Leftover cooked rice to serve

Instructions

1. In a medium bowl, combine the tomato paste, orange juice, cornstarch, water, bouillon powder, tamari, coconut sugar, and hot sauce. Whisk to combine and set aside.

2. Heat the oil in a skillet and sauté the garlic for about 1 minute, or until fragrant. Add the chickpeas and continue to cook for 1–2 minutes.

3. Give the sauce another mix and pour it into the skillet. Bring to a simmer, add the peanut butter, and cook for 1 minute. Then turn off the heat.

4. Serve with rice. Enjoy!

TOMATO PASTE

ORANGE JUICE

CORNSTARCH

VEGGIE BOUILLON POWDER

TAMARI

COCONUT SUGAR

HOT SAUCE

OIL

GARLIC

CHICKPEAS

PEANUT BUTTER

COOKED RICE

EGGPLANT MINI PIZZA

30 minutes, 12 slices

1 large eggplant

1½ Tbsp olive oil

Salt and pepper to taste

1 tsp dried oregano

½ cup (120 g/4.2 oz) tomato sauce
(e.g., marinara or pizza sauce)

2 garlic cloves, minced

¾ cup (90 g/3.2 oz) vegan
mozzarella (page 51)

½ cup (90 g/3.2 oz) cherry
tomatoes, halved

¼ cup (45 g/1.6 oz) olives, sliced

Fresh basil, chopped, for garnish

Instructions

1. Preheat the oven to 425°F (220°C) and line a baking sheet with parchment paper.

2. Slice the eggplant horizontally into ½-inch (1 cm) thick slices. Brush a little olive oil on each side of the slices and place them on the lined baking sheet.

3. Sprinkle them with a little salt, pepper, and half the amount of dried oregano. Bake for 15 minutes.

4. Mix the tomato sauce with the minced garlic, salt, pepper, and the remaining oregano.

5. After 15 minutes, remove the eggplant slices from the oven and top them with the tomato sauce, vegan mozzarella, and any toppings you like (for this dish, I used cherry tomatoes and olives).

6. Bake for a further 10–12 minutes. Garnish with fresh basil and enjoy!

Notes

- **Slice them evenly:** This way, the eggplant pizzas cook at an even rate.

- **Don't underbake the eggplant:** Eggplant can be spongy and rubbery when undercooked.

- **Don't skip the pre-roast:** The first 15 minutes of roasting time are needed to bring out excess water from the eggplant slices and get them to the correct texture.

- **Don't use too many toppings:** Otherwise, the eggplant pizza might turn out soggy.

BUFFALO CHICKPEA TACOS

25 minutes, 4 servings

BUFFALO CHICKPEAS

1 Tbsp vegetable oil

1 medium-sized onion, chopped

1 bell pepper, chopped

2 garlic cloves, minced

1 tsp onion powder

½ tsp garlic powder

½ tsp smoked paprika

½ tsp ground cumin

½ tsp coconut sugar or sweetener of
choice

Salt and black pepper to taste

1 can (425 g/15 oz), chickpeas,
drained and rinsed

½ cup (125 g/4.4 oz) tomato sauce
(passata)

2 Tbsp Sriracha (or more to taste)

2 Tbsp plant-based milk

1 Tbsp balsamic vinegar

OTHER INGREDIENTS

4 small tortillas (gluten-free if needed)
about 6 inches (15 cm) in diameter
(page 52)

1 batch of vegan cheese sauce
(page 31)

Instructions

1. Preheat the oven to 410°F (210°C) and lightly oil a small/medium baking pan.

2. Heat oil in a skillet over medium heat and add the chopped onion and bell pepper. Sauté for 3 minutes, add garlic and all the spices, and cook for a further minute.

3. Add all the remaining ingredients and the chickpeas to the pan and cook over medium-low heat for 2–4 minutes, stirring occasionally, then turn off the heat.

4. Taste the mixture and adjust any seasonings. If you want it spicier, add more Sriracha to your liking.

5. Place the tortillas into the pan and fill them evenly with the chickpea mixture.

6. Drizzle with the vegan cheese sauce or your favorite shredded vegan cheese before baking.

7. Bake in the oven for 10–15 minutes, then enjoy!

CHEESY SPINACH WRAPS WITH RICE

25 minutes, 4 servings

1 Tbsp vegetable oil

½ medium onion, chopped

1 green bell pepper, chopped

½ cup (80 g/2.8 oz) corn (fresh or canned)

2 garlic cloves, minced

1 can (425 g/15 oz) chickpeas, drained and rinsed

½ Tbsp GF soy sauce, tamari, or coconut aminos

½ tsp ground cumin

¼ tsp smoked paprika

¾ tsp salt

Black pepper to taste

3 Tbsp plant-based milk

2 cups (360 g/12.7 oz) cooked leftover rice

1 Tbsp lemon juice

1 batch of vegan cheese sauce (page 31)

4 spinach tortillas (page 56) or tortillas of choice

3–4 Tbsp tomato sauce or Sriracha

Fresh parsley or cilantro, to garnish

Instructions

1. Heat oil in a large skillet and sauté the onion, bell pepper, and corn for about 3–4 minutes. Add the garlic and sauté for a further minute.

2. Add the chickpeas, soy sauce, all spices, and plant-based milk and cook over low-medium heat for a few more minutes, stirring occasionally.

3. Meanwhile, make a batch of the vegan cheese sauce (skip this step if using store-bought cheese).

4. Add the cooked rice and lemon juice to the skillet and stir to combine. Turn off the heat after a few minutes, taste the mixture and adjust any of the seasonings accordingly.

5. Finally, stuff the tortillas with the filling, drizzle with the vegan cheese sauce, tomato sauce (or Sriracha), and garnish with fresh parsley or cilantro. Enjoy!

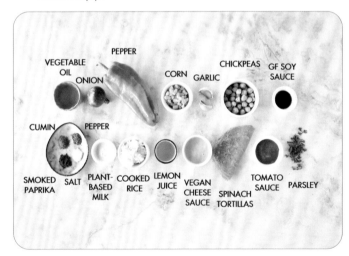

SPAGHETTI MARINARA

30 minutes, 3-4 servings

1 Tbsp olive oil

½ medium onion, diced

⅓ cup (30 g/1.1 oz) carrot, shredded

3 garlic cloves, minced

1 can (800 g/28 oz) crushed
    tomatoes

1 cup (240 g/8.5 oz) passata

1 Tbsp tomato paste

1 tsp dried oregano

¾ tsp salt (or to taste)

Black pepper & red pepper flakes
    to taste

¼ cup fresh basil, chopped

250 g (8.8 oz) spaghetti (gluten-free,
    if needed)

Instructions

1. Heat oil in a large heavy-based pot and sauté the onion and carrot for about 3–4 minutes. Add the garlic and sauté for a further minute.

2. Add all other ingredients, bring the sauce to a boil, reduce the heat to low, and let the sauce simmer for about 20 minutes, stirring occasionally.

3. Meanwhile, cook the spaghetti according to its package directions.

4. Taste the sauce and adjust any of the seasonings to your liking. Pour the sauce over the spaghetti and enjoy!

DESSERTS

OATMEAL CHOCOLATE CHIP BARS

45 minutes, 4 servings

WET INGREDIENTS

1 can (425 g/15 oz) chickpeas, drained and rinsed

½ cup (120 ml/4.2 oz) plant-based milk

1 Tbsp lime juice or lemon juice

⅓ cup (80 g/2.8 oz) cashew butter (or nut/seed butter of choice)

1 tsp vanilla extract

DRY INGREDIENTS

½ cup (100 g/3.5 oz) Erythritol (or granulated sugar of choice)

2 cups (180 g/6.3 oz) quick oats (gluten-free if needed)

1 tsp baking powder

¼ tsp baking soda

¼ tsp salt

½ cup (120 g/4.2 oz) dairy-free chocolate chips + more for the top

Instructions

1. Prepare and measure all the ingredients. I recommend using metric measurements.

2. Preheat the oven to 360°F (180°C) and line a baking pan with parchment paper. My pan measures 9x6 inches (23 x 15 cm).

3. Process all wet ingredients in a food processor until smooth.

4. Add all the dry ingredients (except the chocolate chips) and process again for a few seconds.

5. Then, add the chocolate chips and stir with a spoon.

6. Add the batter to the lined baking pan and top with more chocolate chips or chocolate chunks.

7. Bake in the oven for 28–35 minutes. Insert a toothpick into the middle, and when it comes out dry, the dessert is done!

8. Let it cool and cut into bars. Enjoy! Store leftovers covered in the fridge for up to 4 days or freeze for up to 3 months.

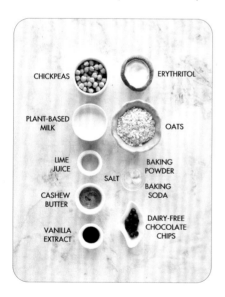

CHICKPEAS ERYTHRITOL

PLANT-BASED MILK OATS

LIME JUICE BAKING POWDER

SALT

CASHEW BUTTER BAKING SODA

VANILLA EXTRACT DAIRY-FREE CHOCOLATE CHIPS

CREAMY BANANA ICE CREAM

10 minutes, 5 servings

5 medium (450 g/15.9 oz) ripe
   bananas

⅓ cup (80 g/2.8 oz) nut/seed butter
   of choice

1–2 Tbsp maple syrup (optional)

Instructions

1. Chop the bananas into 1-inch (2.5 cm) slices and add them to a freezer-safe container (with space in between). Freeze them until solid (at least 1 hour). If you freeze them overnight, let them thaw for about 20 minutes before using.

2. Add the frozen banana pieces, nut/seed butter, and maple syrup (if used) to a high-speed blender. Blend until the mixture is super creamy and lump-free. If your blender has problems blending the mixture, wait a few minutes and try again. It also helps to use a tamper, if the machine has one, to push the ingredients into the blades.

3. Transfer the ice cream back to the freezer-safe container and freeze until it's a scoopable consistency. Enjoy!

Notes

- If you freeze the ice cream overnight, it will be solid. Let it thaw for about 15–20 minutes until it's scoopable.

MARBLE BUNDT CAKE

60 minutes, 10 servings

FLAX EGGS
2 Tbsp ground flax seeds

5 Tbsp water

DRY INGREDIENTS
1 cup (160 g/5.6 oz) rice flour

2 cups (200 g/7.1 oz) oat flour
(gluten-free if needed)

⅓ cup (40 g/1.4 oz) almond flour (or
ground nuts/seeds of choice)

2 tsp baking powder

½ tsp baking soda

WET INGREDIENTS
2 large (225 g/7.9 oz) ripe bananas

⅔ cup (160 ml/5.6 oz) canned
coconut milk (regular or lite)

½ cup (160 g/5.6 oz) maple syrup
(or liquid sweetener of choice)

1 Tbsp lime juice or lemon juice

2 tsp vanilla extract

CHOCOLATE MARBLE
100 g (3.5 oz) dairy-free chocolate,
melted

¼ cup (60 g/2.1 oz) nut butter (or
seed butter of choice)

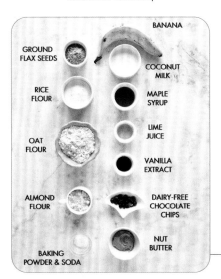

BANANA

GROUND
FLAX SEEDS

COCONUT
MILK

RICE
FLOUR

MAPLE
SYRUP

LIME
JUICE

OAT
FLOUR

VANILLA
EXTRACT

ALMOND
FLOUR

DAIRY-FREE
CHOCOLATE
CHIPS

NUT
BUTTER

BAKING
POWDER & SODA

Instructions

1. I recommend using metric measurements. To make the flax eggs, add 2 Tbsp ground flax seeds (or ground chia seeds) to a small bowl with 5 Tbsp water and stir. Set aside for 5 minutes.

2. Combine all dry ingredients in a bowl and mix with a whisk until there are no lumps.

3. Then blend the wet ingredients in a blender or food processor until completely smooth.

4. Combine the wet and dry ingredients with a whisk. If the batter seems too thick, add another splash of coconut milk.

5. Grease/oil a Bundt cake pan (or cake pan of choice) and preheat the oven to 360°F (180°C).

6. Melt the dairy-free chocolate and nut/seed butter using a double-boiler method or in the microwave. Then add a couple of tablespoons of the cake batter to the chocolate mixture and stir.

7. Spoon the light and dark batters into your cake pan, swapping between each spoonful until there is none left.

8. Bake the cake in the oven for about 40 minutes (+/- 5 minutes) until a toothpick inserted into the thickest part comes out clean. If your cake pan is small and deep, it might take longer. If the pan is large and shallow, the cake might be ready in less time. I used a silicone Bundt cake mold, which measures 9×3 inches (23×7.5 cm).

9. Let the cake cool completely. Drizzle with melted chocolate or peanut butter (optional) and enjoy!

Notes

- Since the batter is oil-free, I use canned coconut milk, which is higher in fat than any other plant-based milk. If you don't like coconut, you can use your favorite plant-based milk and add 2 Tbsp of oil.

- Store leftovers covered in the fridge for up to 4 days or freeze for up to 3 months.

CHOCOLATE MUG CAKE

5 minutes, 1 serving

2 Tbsp gluten-free flour (see notes)

1 ½ Tbsp cocoa powder

1 ½ Tbsp granulated sugar of choice

1 pinch of salt

¼ tsp baking powder

2 Tbsp (30 g/1.1 oz) mashed
banana

3 Tbsp dairy-free milk of choice

¼ tsp vanilla extract

1–2 tsp peanut butter (optional)

Dairy-free chocolate chips (optional)

GF FLOUR

BANANA

COCOA
POWDER

DAIRY-FREE
MILK

COCONUT
SUGAR

VANILLA
EXTRACT

BAKING
POWDER

PEANUT
BUTTER

SALT

DAIRY-FREE
CHOCOLATE
CHIPS

Instructions

1. Add all the dry ingredients (flour, cocoa powder, coconut sugar, salt, and baking powder) to a mug and stir.

2. Mash a banana with a fork in a bowl or plate. You need 2 Tbsp of mashed banana for this recipe.

3. Then add all the wet ingredients (mashed banana, dairy-free milk, vanilla extract) to the mug and stir to combine. You can optionally add 1–2 tsp of peanut butter (or nut/seed butter of choice) into the middle and push it down slightly with a spoon for a "hidden center."

4. Microwave for 60–70 seconds for a fudgy texture, or 80–90 seconds for a lighter, cakier texture. *The time varies based on your microwave, the size/shape of the mug, and the flour you use. I recommend microwaving it for 60 seconds, testing it with a spoon, and continuing in 10-second increments until it reaches your desired consistency. Enjoy!*

Notes

- **Flour:** I use a gluten-free flour blend of 50% white rice flour, 30% chickpea flour, and 20% tapioca flour. An all-purpose GF flour blend (e.g., Bob's Red Mill) should work too. If you aren't gluten-free, you can use regular all-purpose flour.

- **Oven method:** I recommend using an oven-safe ramekin and baking it at 350°F (177°C). First, check it with a toothpick inserted into the center at 12 minutes, then every couple of minutes after until it reaches your desired consistency.

HOMEMADE MARZIPAN

5 minutes, 4 servings

¾ cup + 1 Tbsp (90 g/3.2 oz)
   blanched almond flour

9 Tbsp (70 g/2.5 oz) powdered
   sugar or powdered Erythritol

1½ Tbsp (20 ml/0.7 oz) water or a
   liquid sweetener (see notes)

¼–½ tsp almond extract (optional but
   highly recommended)

½ tsp rose water, food-grade
   (optional)

Instructions

1. I recommend using metric measurements. First, process the almond flour and powdered sugar (I use Erythritol, which I process in an electric coffee/spice grinder until powdery) in a food processor.

2. Add the water (or your favorite liquid sweetener), almond extract, and rose water (optional) and pulse a few times until the dough holds together and forms a ball. If the dough is too dry, add more water (or syrup). Add just a little at a time until a thick dough forms. If it's too sticky/wet, add more almond flour.

3. Knead the marzipan ball on a clean surface for about 30 seconds. You can now shape it into a log, wrap it up in cling wrap, and refrigerate it. It will firm up slightly in the fridge.

Notes

- **Water or liquid sweetener:** If you have a sweet tooth, use a liquid sweetener for sweeter marzipan.

- The recipe makes a small batch of 185 grams (6.5 oz), but you can double the recipe for a larger batch.

- If you use agave syrup or corn syrup, you should be able to store it in the fridge for up to 2–3 weeks (probably even longer) or up to 3 months in the freezer. If you use water, use it within a week.

PEANUT BUTTER TRUFFLES

20 minutes, 12 truffles

PB FILLING

⅔ cup (160 g/5.6 oz) peanut butter
(or sunflower seed butter)

3 Tbsp (60 g/2.1 oz) maple syrup (or
liquid sweetener of choice)

4–5 Tbsp coconut flour (see
instructions)

½ tsp vanilla extract

⅛ tsp salt

CHOCOLATE

⅔ cup (120 g/4.2 oz) dairy-free
chocolate chips

½ tsp coconut oil (optional)

PEANUT BUTTER

MAPLE SYRUP

COCONUT FLOUR

VANILLA EXTRACT

SALT

DAIRY-FREE CHOCOLATE CHIPS

COCONUT OIL

Instructions

1. Process all the PB filling ingredients in a food processor for a couple of seconds until the mixture is combined. Depending on the type of peanut butter, you might need to add more or less coconut flour. If it's drippy, you will need about 5 tablespoons. If it's firm, you will need about 4 tablespoons (or less). The dough should be soft but not sticky (see notes).

2. With your hands, roll 1 Tbsp (20 grams) portions of the mixture into balls and place them onto a lined baking sheet (cookie sheet) or plate. I had enough dough for 12 balls. Freeze for about 30–45 minutes.

3. To make the chocolate coating, simply melt the chocolate chips with the coconut oil in a double boiler or the microwave.

4. Dip each ball into the melted chocolate. Remove it with a fork and let the excess chocolate drip off. Then place each chocolate-covered ball onto a baking sheet lined with wax paper (or parchment paper) and let it harden.

5. Chill before serving and enjoy!

Notes

- If the mixture is a little dry, add more maple syrup or plant-based milk a spoonful at a time. If it's too wet, add extra coconut flour or allow the mixture to chill in the fridge for 1 hour or so to firm up.

- Store the leftovers covered in the fridge for up to 1 week.

PEANUT BUTTER COOKIES

25 minutes, 6 cookies

COOKIES

2 Tbsp ground flax seeds + 6 Tbsp water

½ cup (60 g/2.1 oz) ground nuts/seeds of choice

2 Tbsp (20 g/0.7 oz) coconut flour (see notes)

1 tsp baking powder

3 Tbsp granulated sugar of choice

3 Tbsp (48 g/1.7 oz) peanut butter (or sunflower seed butter)

1 tsp vanilla extract

½ Tbsp coconut oil

ADD-INS (OPTIONAL)

Dairy-free chocolate chips

Instructions

1. Preheat the oven to 350°F (177°C) and line a cookie sheet with parchment paper.

2. Add the ground flax seeds and water to a bowl, whisk, and set aside for 5 minutes.

3. Next, add the dry ingredients to a bowl and whisk. Then, add the wet ingredients and mix with a hand mixer or spoon. If the dough appears too dry, add a little more water or plant-based milk. You can optionally add 1 ½–2 tablespoons of chocolate chips, raisins, or nuts/seeds.

4. Scoop heaped tablespoon portions of the dough and roll them into balls using your hands. Place the dough balls onto your lined baking tray.

5. Gently flatten each dough ball and bake them for 13–16 minutes. This recipe makes just a small batch of 6 cookies.

6. Let them cool completely and enjoy.

Notes

- **Flax:** You can use ground chia seeds instead of flax seeds. Half of a large banana (mashed) or ¼ cup of applesauce should also work fine.

- **Coconut flour:** If you don't have coconut flour, you can use the double amount of a different flour, (e.g., 4 tablespoons of oat flour or almond flour).

- Store any leftover cookies in an airtight container on the counter for a few days or in the fridge for up to 1 week.

FUDGY CHOCOLATE COOKIES

25 minutes, 8–10 cookies

1 ½ Tbsp ground chia seeds + ¼ cup (60 g/2.1 oz) water

1 scant cup (100 g/3.5 oz) ground sunflower seeds or almond flour

⅜ cup (75 g/2.6 oz) granulated sugar of choice

5 Tbsp (30 g/1.1 oz) cocoa powder

1 tsp baking powder

¼ tsp salt

¼ tsp espresso powder (optional but recommended)

3 ½ Tbsp (50 g/1.8 oz) nut/seed butter of choice

1 ½ Tbsp (18 g/0.6 oz) coconut oil, melted

1 tsp vanilla extract

⅓ cup (60 g/2.1 oz) dairy-free chocolate chips

Instructions

1. I recommend using metric measurements. First, add ground chia seeds and water to a small bowl, whisk, and set aside for 5 minutes. Also, preheat the oven to 350°F (177°C) and line a baking sheet with parchment paper.

2. To a medium-sized bowl (or food processor), add the ground sunflower seeds (or almond flour), your granulated sugar of choice, cocoa powder, baking powder, salt, and espresso powder. Mix until there are no lumps.

3. Then, add your nut/seed butter of choice, coconut oil, vanilla extract, and the chia seed mixture. Stir (or blend, if using a food processor) until combined.

4. Finally, add the dairy-free chocolate chips (or chopped chocolate) and mix with your hands until you have a smooth dough.

5. Divide the dough into 8 pieces (each weighing about 50 grams, or make 10 smaller ones) and roll each piece with your hands into a ball. You can also use an ice cream scoop.

6. Place the cookie dough balls on the prepared parchment paper and flatten them with your hand. Bake in the oven for 14–16 minutes. They will be soft when you take them out but will firm up once cooled. Enjoy! Store any leftover cookies in an airtight container on the counter for a few days or in the fridge for up to 1 week.

THUMBPRINT COOKIES

25 minutes, 14 cookies

1⅛ cups (125 g/4.4 oz) almond flour
    (or ground sunflower seeds)

4 Tbsp (32 g/1.1 oz) tapioca flour/
    starch (or arrowroot flour)

3 Tbsp (40 g/1.4 oz) granulated
    sugar of choice (I used Erythritol)

1 tsp baking powder

¼ cup (64 g/2.3 oz) cashew butter
    or almond butter, or tahini (runny,
    not firm)

1 tsp vanilla extract

1–2 Tbsp cold water + more,
    if needed

4 tsp maple syrup

Jam of choice (I used homemade
    raspberry, page 47)

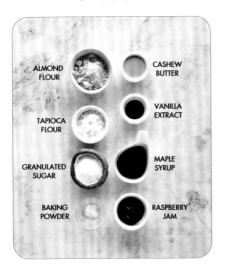

Instructions

1. Add all the dry ingredients (almond flour, tapioca flour/starch, sugar, and baking powder) to a bowl and stir with a spoon.

2. Then, add the cashew butter, vanilla extract, maple syrup, and 1 tablespoon of cold water. First, stir with a spoon, then use your hands to shape the dough into a ball. If the dough is crumbly, add more water, 1 teaspoon at a time. If the dough is a little sticky at first, let it rest for a couple of minutes or add more flour. **Note:** The nut/seed butter should be runny, not firm. If yours is firm, I recommend heating it in a double boiler with a few drops of oil.

3. Shape the dough into 14 balls and place them on a cookie sheet lined with parchment paper or a silicone mat.

4. Make an indentation in each ball using your thumb or a ½ tsp measuring spoon.

5. Fill ½ tsp of jam into each indentation, then transfer the cookie sheet to the fridge and chill for at least 30 minutes (or overnight).

6. Preheat the oven to 350°F (177°C) and bake the cookies for about 12–15 minutes, or until slightly golden brown. Enjoy! Store any leftover cookies in an airtight container on the counter for a few days or in the fridge for up to 1 week.

ZUCCHINI BROWNIES

45 minutes, 8 brownies

DRY INGREDIENTS

¾ cup (150 g/5.3 oz) granulated
   sweetener of choice

1½ cups (135 g/4.8 oz) oat flour
   (gluten-free if needed)

½ cup + 1 Tbsp (50 g/1.8 oz) cocoa
   powder, unsweetened

1 tsp baking powder

¼ tsp baking soda

⅓ tsp salt

1 tsp instant coffee powder (optional)

½ cup (90 g/3.2 oz) dairy-free
   chocolate chips or chunks

WET INGREDIENTS

1¼ cups (200 g/7.1 oz) shredded
   zucchini tightly packed

½ cup (120 g/4.2 oz) nut/seed
   butter of choice (or ¼ cup oil)

¼ cup (60 ml/2.1 oz) plant-based milk

1 tsp vanilla extract

Instructions

1. I recommend using metric measurements. Line a 6x9 inch (15x23 cm) or slightly larger pan with parchment paper, or grease it with vegan butter or oil. Also, preheat the oven to 360°F (180°C).

2. Process all the dry ingredients (except the chocolate chips) in a food processor.

3. Then, add the wet ingredients and blend again until the batter is smooth. Finally, add the chocolate chips and stir with a spoon.

4. Pour the batter into the pan and add more chocolate chips on top.

5. Bake in the oven for between 30–40 minutes. For fudgy brownies, I recommend 30 minutes (or slightly less). For cakey brownies, I recommend 40 minutes or a little more. Insert a toothpick into the center of a brownie after 30 minutes, and if it comes out clean/slightly crumbly, the brownies are done. If the toothpick comes out wet, they need more baking time.

6. Let the brownies cool completely. They firm up once they cool and taste even better on day 2! Enjoy! Store leftovers covered in the fridge for up to 4 days or freeze for up to 2 months.

NO-BAKE CHEESECAKE

30 minutes, 8 slices

CRUST

½ cup (75 g/2.6 oz) nuts or seeds
    of choice
1 cup (90 g/3.2 oz) oats
    (gluten-free if needed)
150 g (5.3 oz) pitted dates
1 tsp vanilla extract
½ Tbsp coconut oil

CREAM

⅔ cup (100 g/3.5 oz) cashews,
    soaked
1 cup (240 ml/8.5 oz) canned
    coconut milk
3 Tbsp (60 g/2.1 oz) maple syrup
    or any other liquid sweetener
1 tsp vanilla extract
2 Tbsp lemon juice or lime juice
3 tsp pink dragon fruit powder
    (optional)
1½ tsp agar powder (not flakes)
¼ cup (60 ml/2.1 oz) water

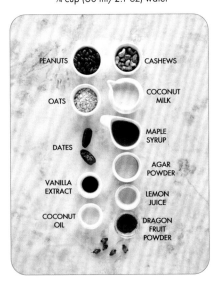

Instructions

1. I recommend using metric measurements. Start by soaking the cashews in hot water for an hour or boiling them for 15 minutes (or leave them in cold water overnight).

2. Process all the crust ingredients in a food processor until the mixture holds together when you press it between your fingers. Press the dough into the bottom and sides of a greased 6-inch springform pan, then transfer it to the fridge.

3. Blend all cream ingredients, except the agar powder and water, in a blender (or powerful food processor) for 1–2 minutes or until the cream is completely smooth.

4. Add the agar powder and water to a saucepan. Bring the mixture to a boil and let it simmer for 3 minutes, stirring frequently. Immediately add the mixture to the blender and blend again for 10–20 seconds to combine.

5. Quickly pour the cream over the crust. Refrigerate for a few hours (or overnight) until set. To speed up the process, transfer the pan to the freezer for 45–60 minutes, or until set. The cheesecake tastes best when it's served cold but not frozen.

Notes

- **Crust:** As it's not baked, this crust is soft. If you prefer it to be firmer, bake the crust in the oven for 15–20 minutes at 350°F (177°C). Let it cool completely before you add the cheesecake layer.

- **Agar powder:** Please use agar powder and not agar flakes. This ingredient cannot be omitted because it acts as a thickener.

- Store leftovers covered in the fridge for up to 5 days.

BLUEBERRY APPLE CRUMBLE

40 minutes, 8 servings

FRUIT MIXTURE

2 large (400 g/14.1 oz) apples,
  cored and chopped

3 cups (500 g/17.6 oz) blueberries,
  fresh or frozen

5 Tbsp (62 g/2.2 oz) coconut sugar
  or brown sugar (or Erythritol)

2 Tbsp cornstarch or arrowroot flour

1 tsp vanilla extract

1 Tbsp lemon juice

1 tsp cinnamon

STREUSEL/CRUMBLE

1 cup (90 g/3.2 oz) oat flour
  (gluten-free if needed)

½ heaped cup (60 g/2.1 oz) almond
  flour (or any ground nuts/seeds)

4 Tbsp (50 g/1.8 oz) coconut sugar
  or brown sugar (or Erythritol)

5 Tbsp (40 g/1.4 oz) tapioca flour or
  arrowroot flour

4 Tbsp (50 g/1.8 oz) coconut oil
  (see notes)

1 tsp vanilla extract

Instructions

1. I recommend using the metric measurements. Preheat the oven to 360°F (180°C).

2. Chop the apples and transfer them to a large bowl with the blueberries.

3. Add the sugar, cornstarch, vanilla extract, lemon juice, and cinnamon. Stir to combine.

4. Transfer the fruit mixture to a baking pan (e.g., 8x8 inches/20x20 cm).

5. For the streusel, add the dry ingredients to a mixing bowl and stir with a spoon. Then, add the coconut oil and vanilla extract and mix everything with your hands until crumbly. If it's too dry, add a little more oil or water.

6. Sprinkle the streusel over the fruit mixture. Finally, bake the crumble in the oven for 30 minutes, or until the top is golden. Enjoy warm alone or with vegan custard or ice cream!

Notes

- **For an oil-free recipe,** use 5 Tbsp of runny nut/seed butter (e.g., cashew butter, coconut butter, almond butter, sunflower seed butter).

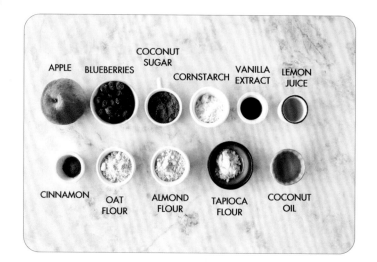

COFFEE CHOCOLATE PUDDING

5 minutes, 2 servings

80 g (2.8 oz) dairy-free chocolate

1 package (350 g/12.3 oz) silken
  tofu (see notes)

2½ Tbsp (50 g/1.8 oz) maple syrup
  or liquid sweetener of choice

1 tsp instant coffee granules, mixed
  with 1 tsp hot water to make a paste

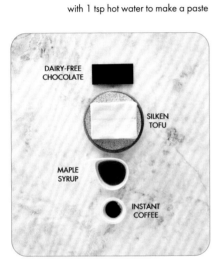

Instructions

1. First, melt the chocolate in a double boiler on the stove (or in the microwave).

2. Blend the drained silken tofu and maple syrup first. Then add the melted chocolate and coffee, blending again until super creamy.

3. Pour the chocolate coffee cream into small jars, refrigerate for about 1 hour, and enjoy!

Notes

- **Silken tofu:** Use vegan cream cheese or avocado for a soy-free pudding.

- **For a fluffier pudding/mousse**, whip up ¼ cup of aquafaba (the liquid from a can of unsalted chickpeas or from cooking dried chickpeas) and then fold it into the chocolate cream.

FRUITY CHERRY PIE

40 minutes, 8 slices

CRUST

½ cup (100 g/3.5 oz) pitted dates, soaked

⅔ cup (90 g/3.2 oz) sunflower seeds or nuts of choice

1 cup (90 g/3.2 oz) oats (gluten-free, if needed)

1 tsp vanilla extract

1 pinch of salt

CHERRY FILLING

2 cups (300 g/10.6 oz) pitted cherries (I used canned, unsweetened)

¼ cup (85 g/3 oz) maple syrup

⅔ cup (160 g/5.6 oz) cherry juice, unsweetened

½ Tbsp vanilla extract

2½ Tbsp (20 g/0.7 oz) arrowroot flour, tapioca flour, or cornstarch

OPTIONAL TOPPING

Coconut whipped cream, to serve

Instructions

1. Preheat the oven to 360°F (180°C) and line a 7-inch springform pan with parchment paper.

2. To make the crust, process all the crust ingredients in a food processor. The dough should stick together when pressed between your fingers.

3. Press the dough evenly into the bottom and sides of the springform pan and set it aside.

4. To make the filling, combine the filling ingredients in a medium saucepan and stir well until the starch dissolves. Bring the mixture to a simmer, stirring frequently, until it thickens considerably.

5. Transfer the cherry filling to the prepared crust and bake for 25 minutes, or until the crust has browned. Cool the pie completely before serving. Enjoy with a dollop of coconut whipped cream. Store leftovers covered in the fridge for up to 5 days.

DATES SUNFLOWER SEEDS OATS VANILLA EXTRACT SALT

CHERRIES MAPLE SYRUP CHERRY JUICE VANILLA EXTRACT ARROWROOT FLOUR

NO-BAKE BROWNIE BITES

10 minutes, 16 mini brownies

DRY INGREDIENTS

½ cup (70 g/2.5 oz) sunflower seeds

¼ cup (30 g/1.1 oz) walnuts (or
   nuts/seeds of choice)

⅓ cup (25 g/0.9 oz) cocoa powder

1 pinch of salt

WET INGREDIENTS

¾ cup (150 g/5.3 oz) pitted dates
   (see notes)

1 tsp vanilla extract

OPTIONAL TOPPING

Chocolate Spread (page 44)

Instructions

1. Process all the dry ingredients in a food processor, add the dates and vanilla extract, then blend until the dough sticks together when pressed between your fingers.

2. Line a 5-inch square baking pan (double the recipe if you have an 8-inch baking pan) with parchment paper and leave about a 2-inch overhang on both sides. Grease the paper with a bit of oil.

3. Transfer the brownie dough to the pan and press it down firmly.

4. Optionally, make my chocolate spread (page 44) and thin it with water into a glaze consistency.

5. Pour the glaze over the brownie dough and transfer the pan to the freezer for about 1 hour to set.

6. Cut into 16 equal brownie bites and enjoy!

Notes

- If the dates aren't soft or moist enough, soak them in warm water until they are soft.

- Store leftovers covered in the fridge for up to 1 week or freeze for up to 3 months.

THANK YOU

Thank you to my dear sister Katrin, who was the reason I stopped eating meat in the first place. Without you, Katrin, this vegan cookbook probably wouldn't exist!

Another big thank you goes to my parents, who accepted that I stopped eating meat when I was six years old and didn't force me to change my mind. My parents have always believed in my dreams and supported me no matter what decisions I made, no matter how crazy they were. For that, I thank you, mom and dad.

A big thank you to my partner Wolfgang, who went vegan with me in September 2011 and has since tried all my food creations, including the sweet ones (even though he doesn't like desserts!). Thank you for buying all the ingredients for my recipes, doing the dishes, and supporting me!

Of course, I also want to thank the *ElaVegan* community on social media (especially Instagram) and my blog visitors, who never fail to put a smile on my face with their sweet comments, private messages, and photos of the recipes they recreate every day. Thank you so much for your support!

ABOUT THE AUTHOR

Ela is a passionate food blogger, recipe writer, food photographer, and the creator of *ElaVegan*.com. She loves to cook healthy, vegan food that is also gluten-free. In 2015, her creativity led her to Instagram, where she began spreading her passion for healthy plant-based dishes. She has helped many people transition to veganism with her recipes, something that is truly near and dear to her heart. At first, she started posting her recipes in Instagram captions, but once her Instagram family grew, people asked for a food blog, where all her recipes could be bundled in one easily searchable place. At the end of 2016, the *ElaVegan* blog went live, and it turned out to be more successful than she could ever have imagined.

In 2019/2020, Ela started getting more and more messages, comments, and emails from her Instagram community, asking if she could turn her recipes into a cookbook. And it's finally here...her first cookbook!

INDEX

Mango Publishing, established in 2014, publishes an eclectic list of books by diverse authors—both new and established voices—on topics ranging from business, personal growth, women's empowerment, LGBTQ+ studies, health, and spirituality to history, popular culture, time management, decluttering, lifestyle, mental wellness, aging, and sustainable living. We were recently named 2019 *and* 2020's #1 fastest-growing independent publisher by *Publishers Weekly*. Our success is driven by our main goal, which is to publish high-quality books that will entertain readers as well as make a positive difference in their lives.

Our readers are our most important resource; we value your input, suggestions, and ideas. We'd love to hear from you—after all, we are publishing books for you!

Please stay in touch with us and follow us at:

Facebook: Mango Publishing
Twitter: @MangoPublishing
Instagram: @MangoPublishing
LinkedIn: Mango Publishing
Pinterest: Mango Publishing
Newsletter: mangopublishinggroup.com/newsletter

Join us on Mango's journey to reinvent publishing, one book at a time.